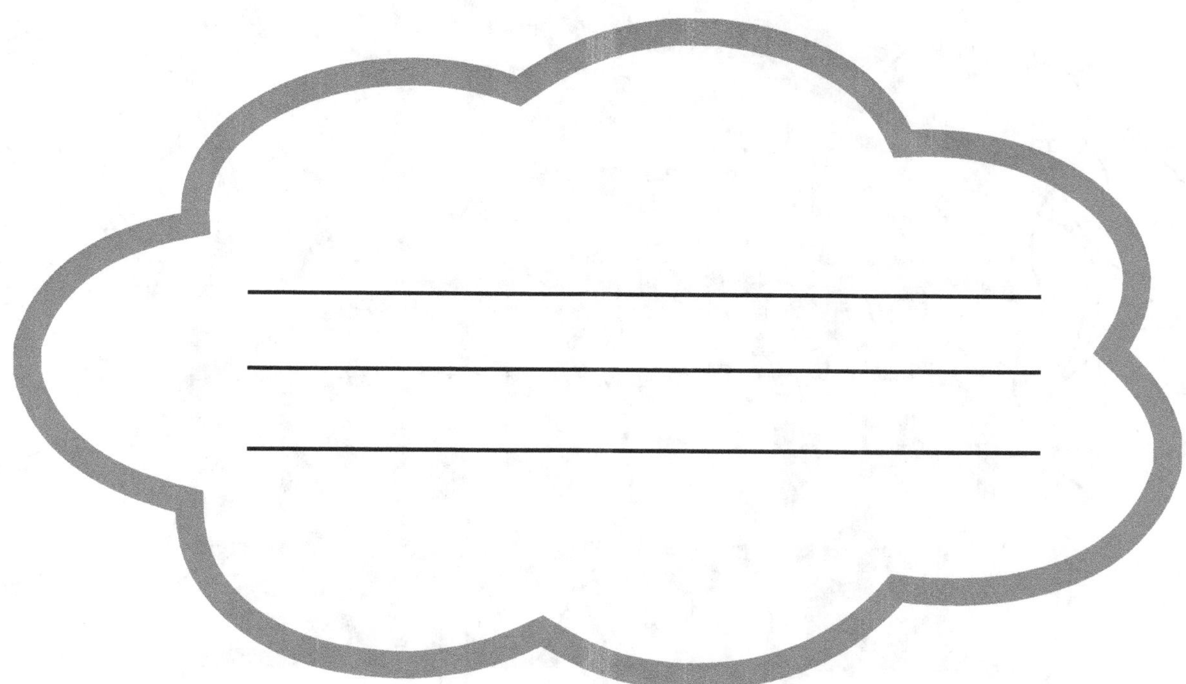

© 2023, Al&Vy Published
God Bless You Inspirational Coloring Book

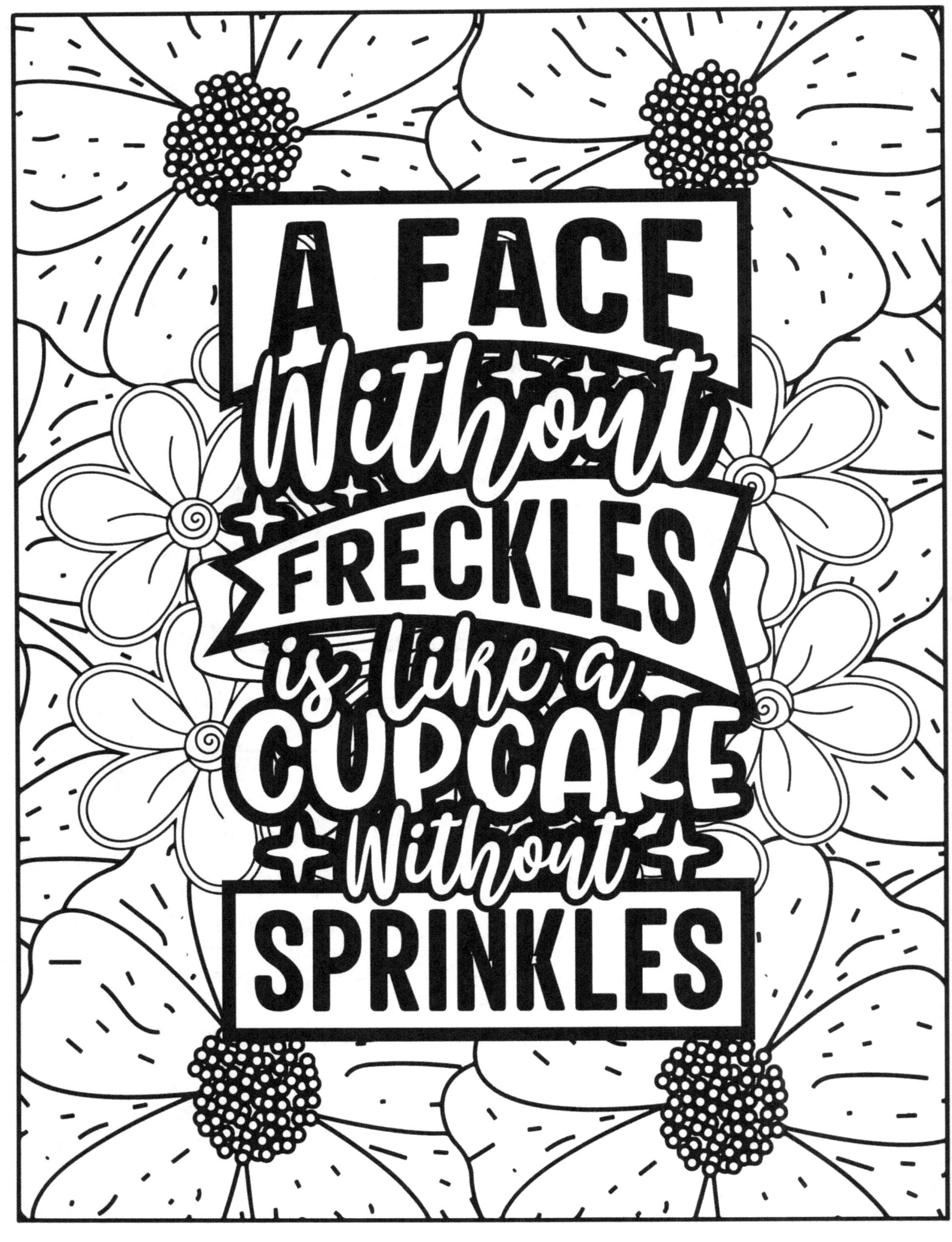

A FACE
Without
FRECKLES
is like a
CUPCAKE
Without
SPRINKLES

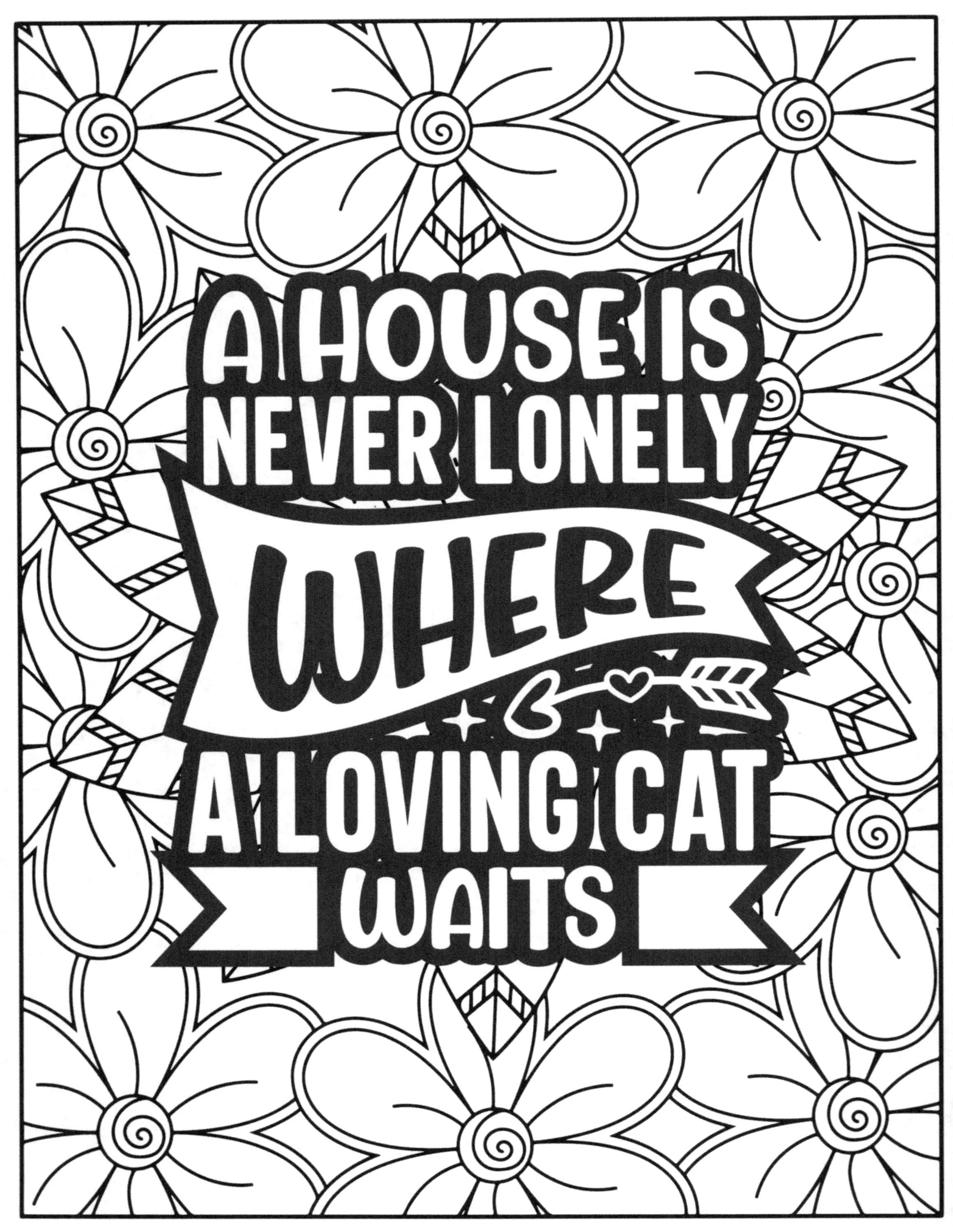

A HOUSE IS NEVER LONELY
WHERE
A LOVING CAT WAITS

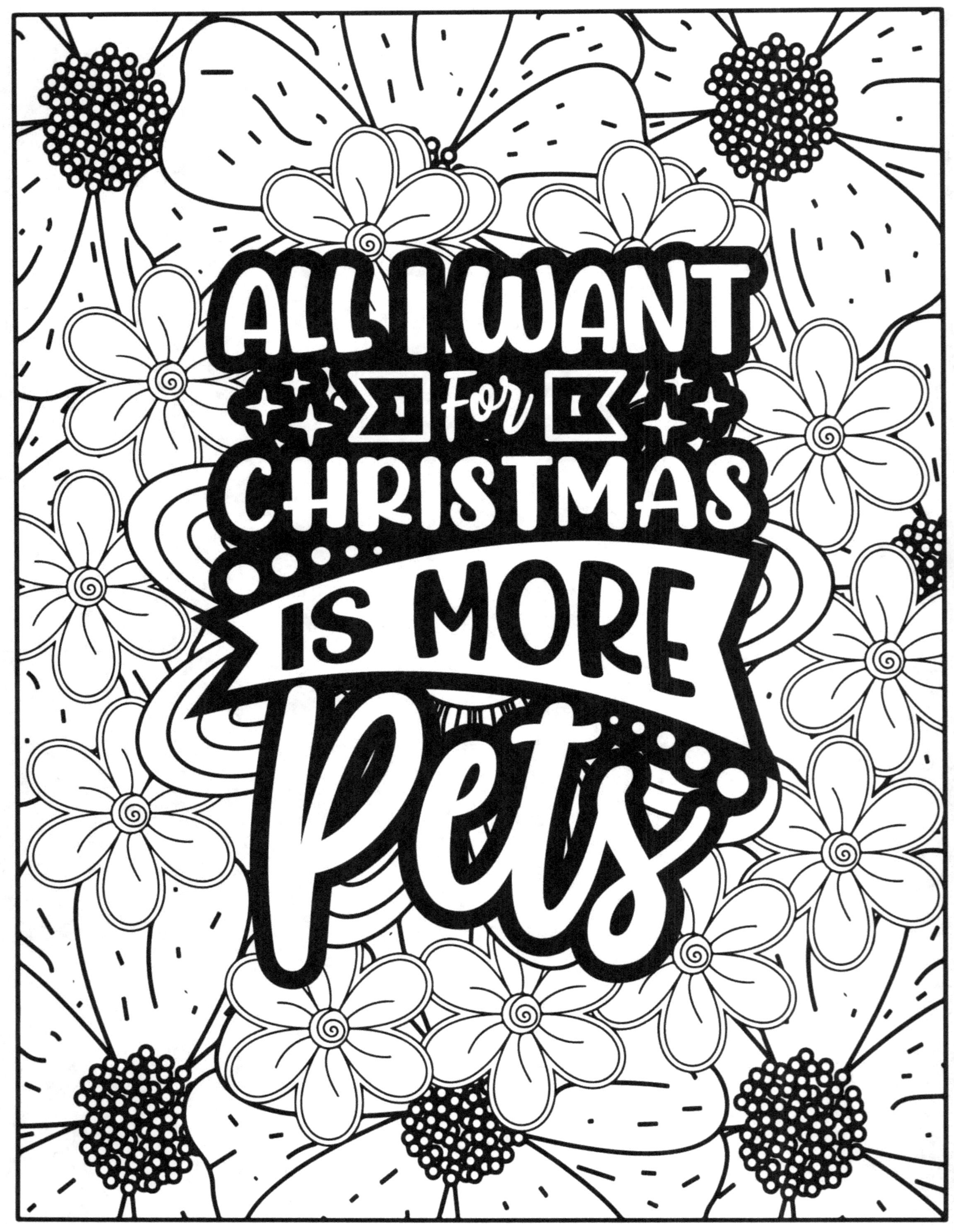

ALL I WANT
FOR
CHRISTMAS
IS MORE
Pets

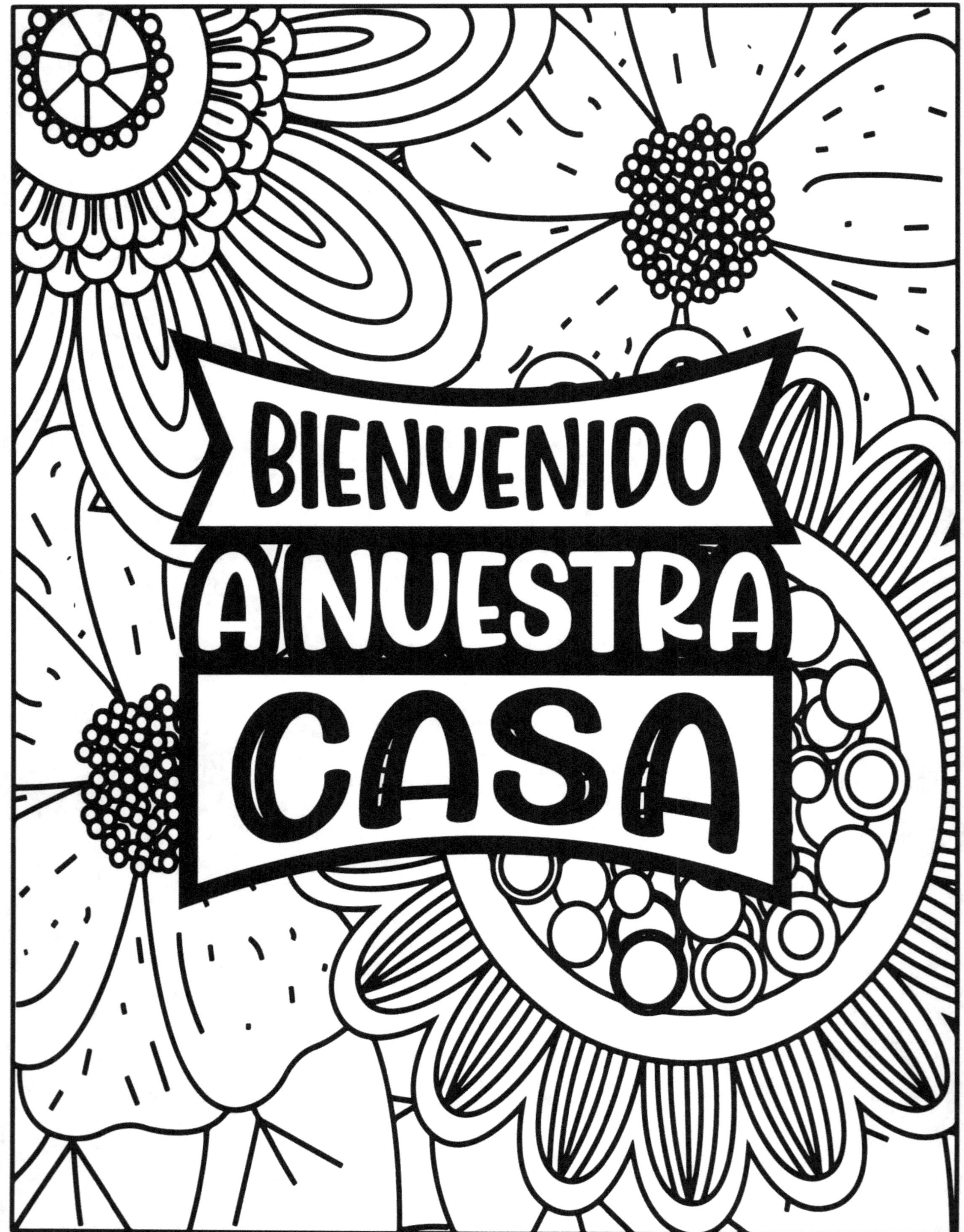

BIENVENIDO
A NUESTRA
CASA

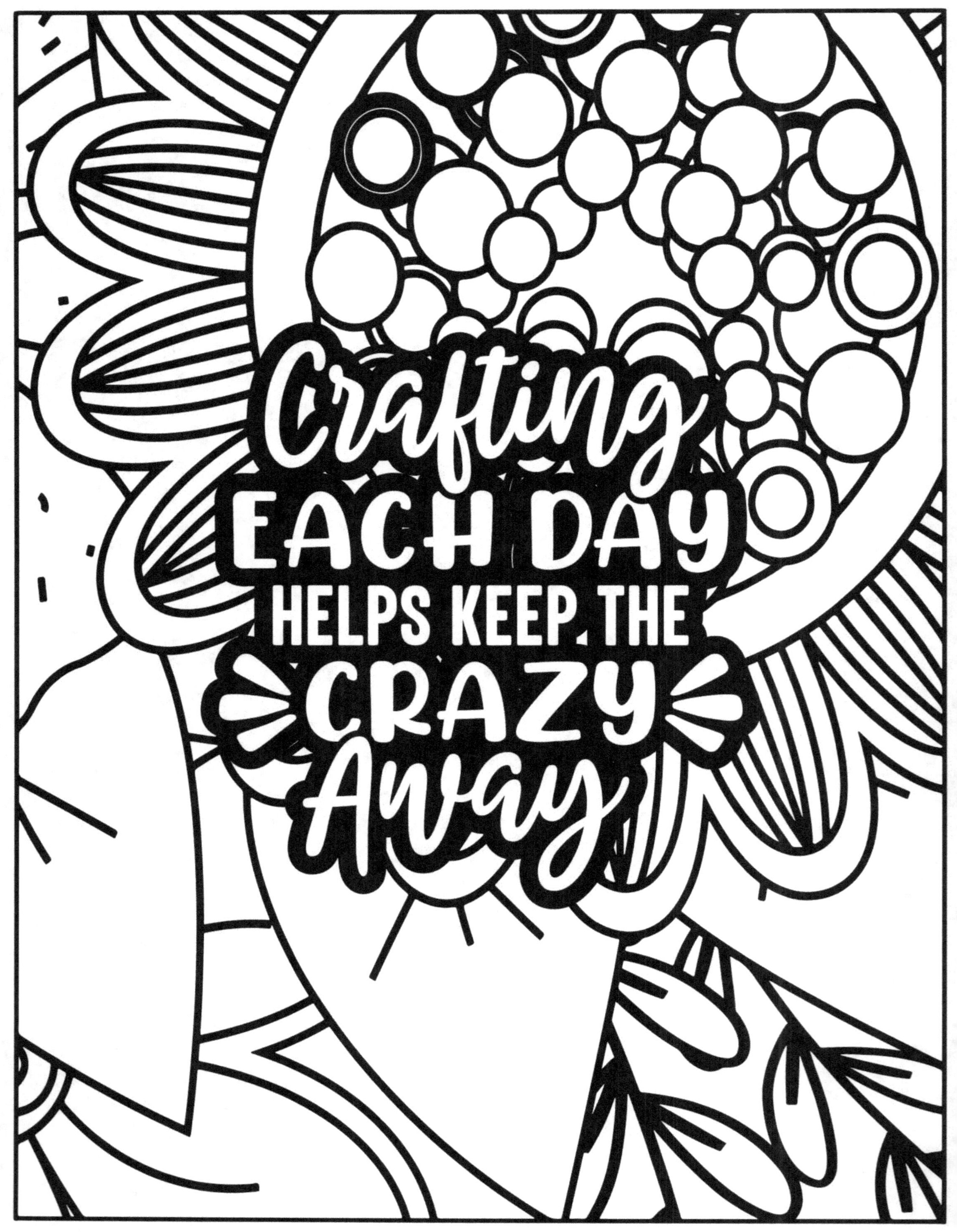

Crafting
EACH DAY
HELPS KEEP. THE
CRAZY
Away

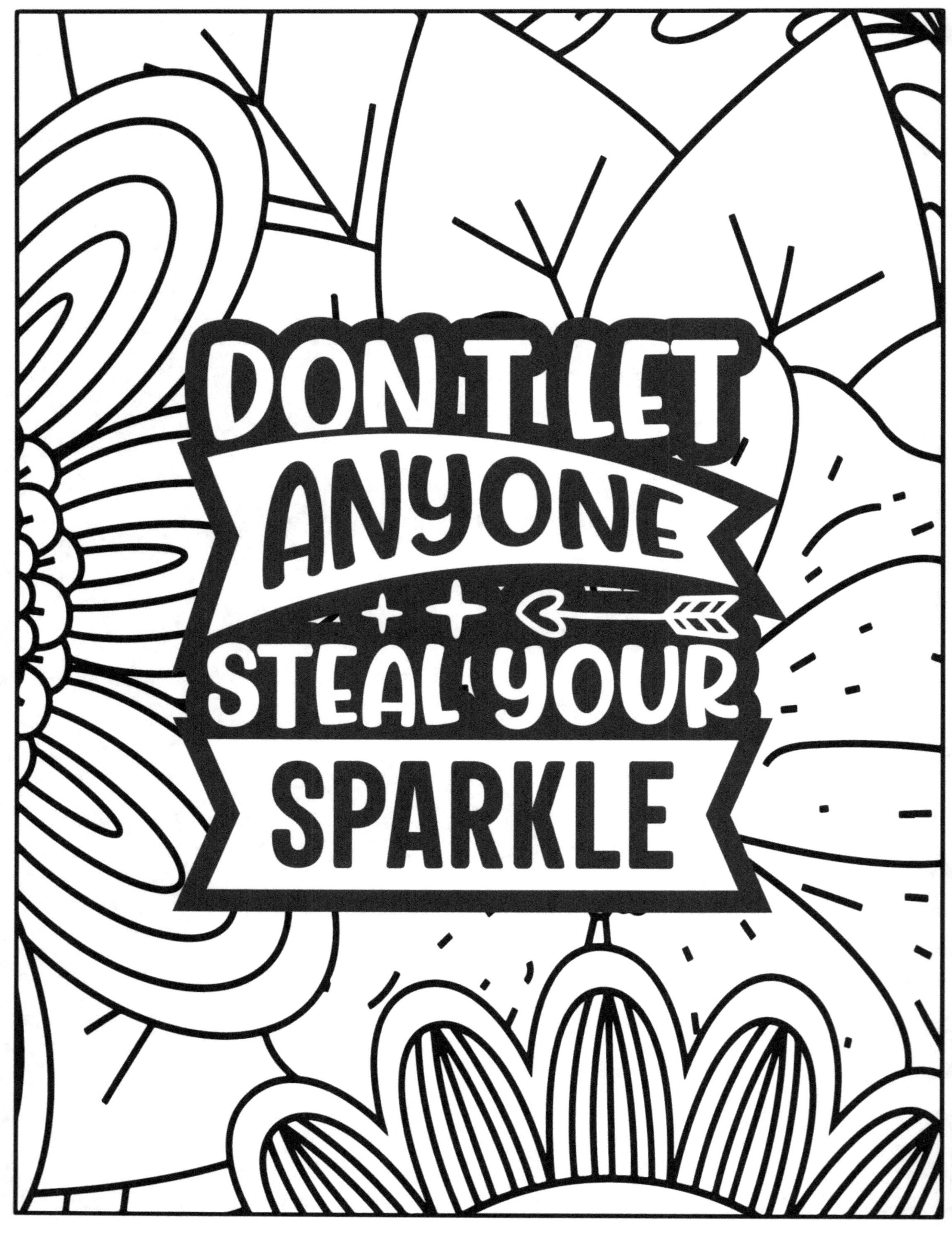

DON'T LET
ANYONE
STEAL YOUR
SPARKLE

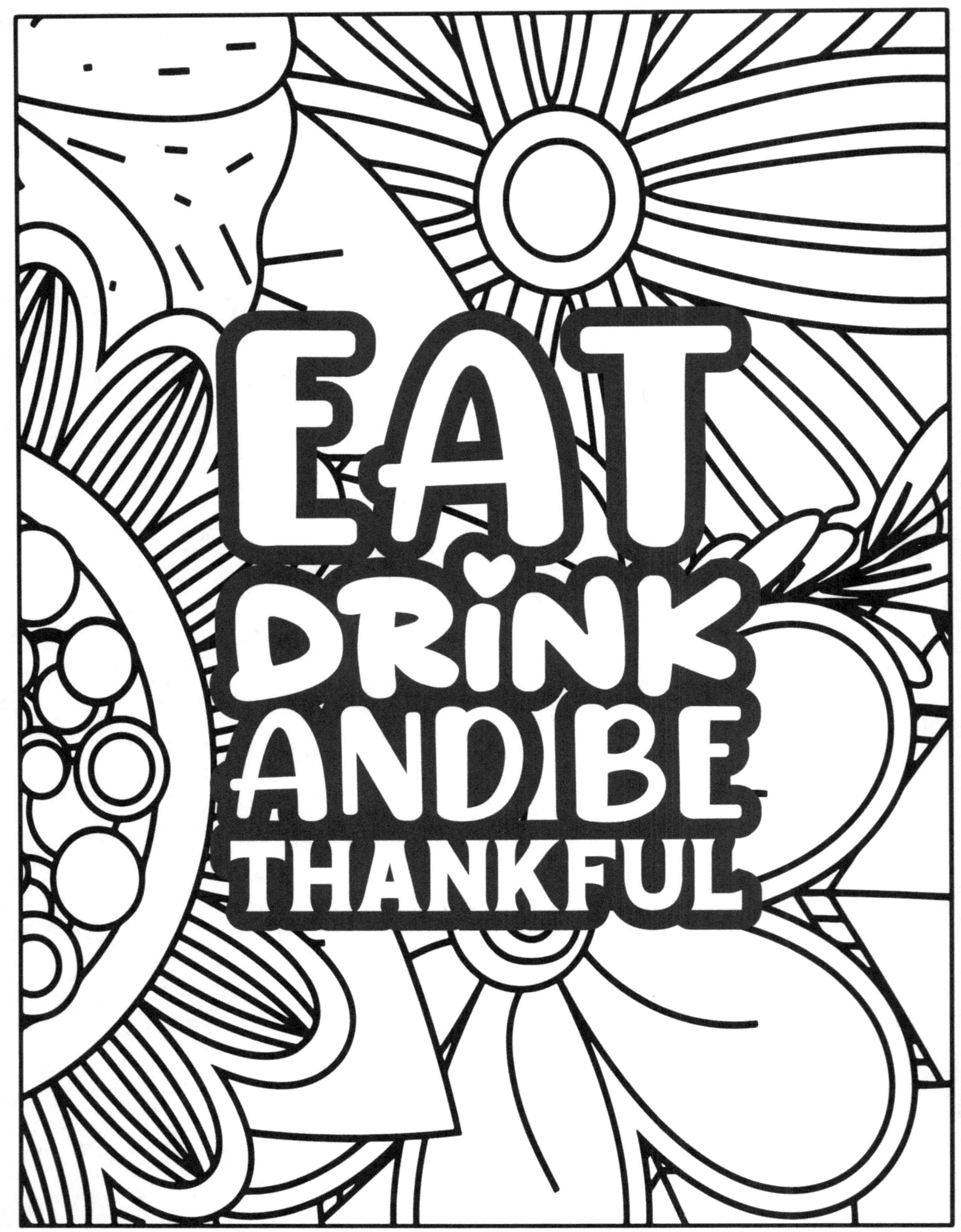
EAT
DRINK
AND BE
THANKFUL

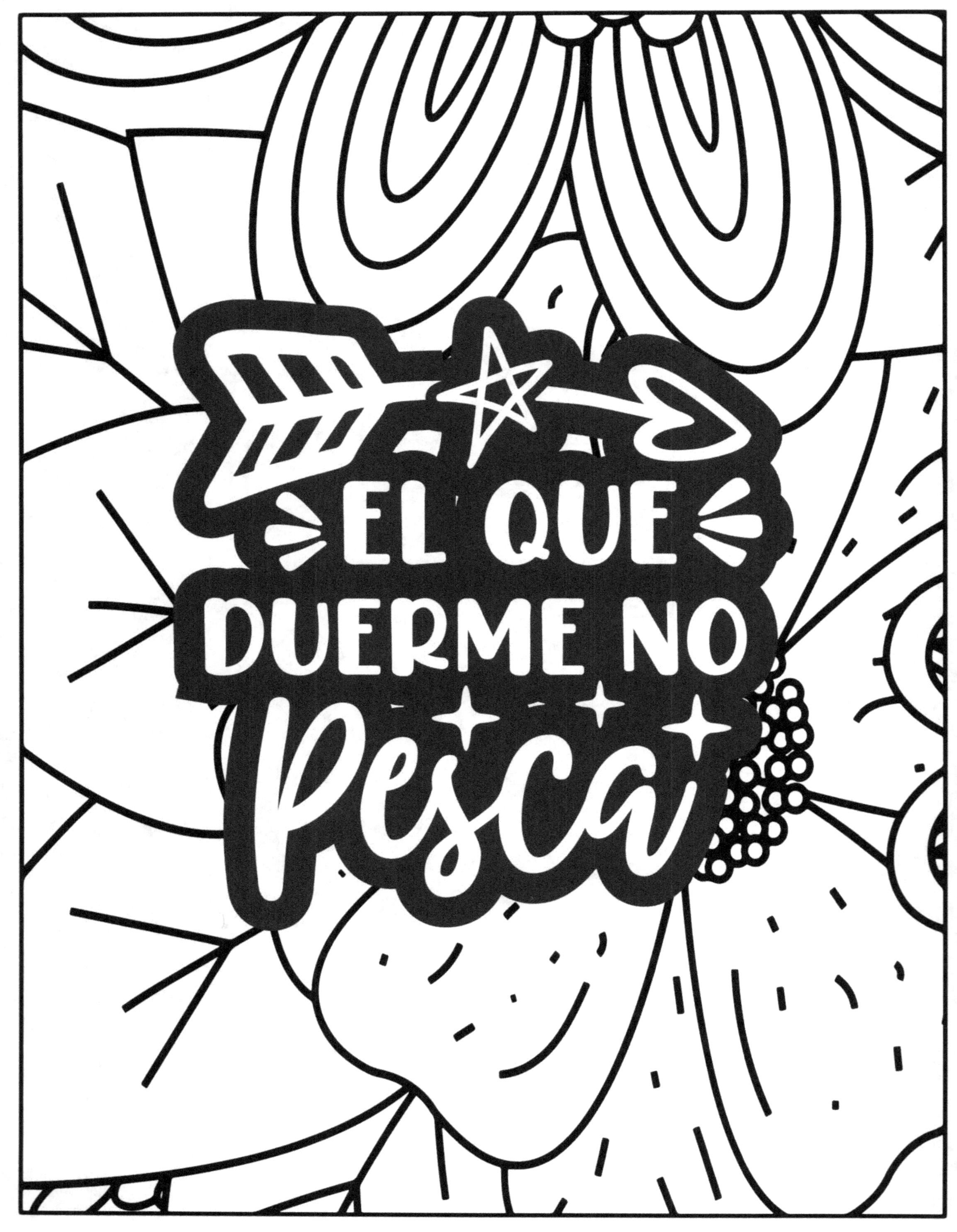

EL QUE
DUERME NO
Pesca

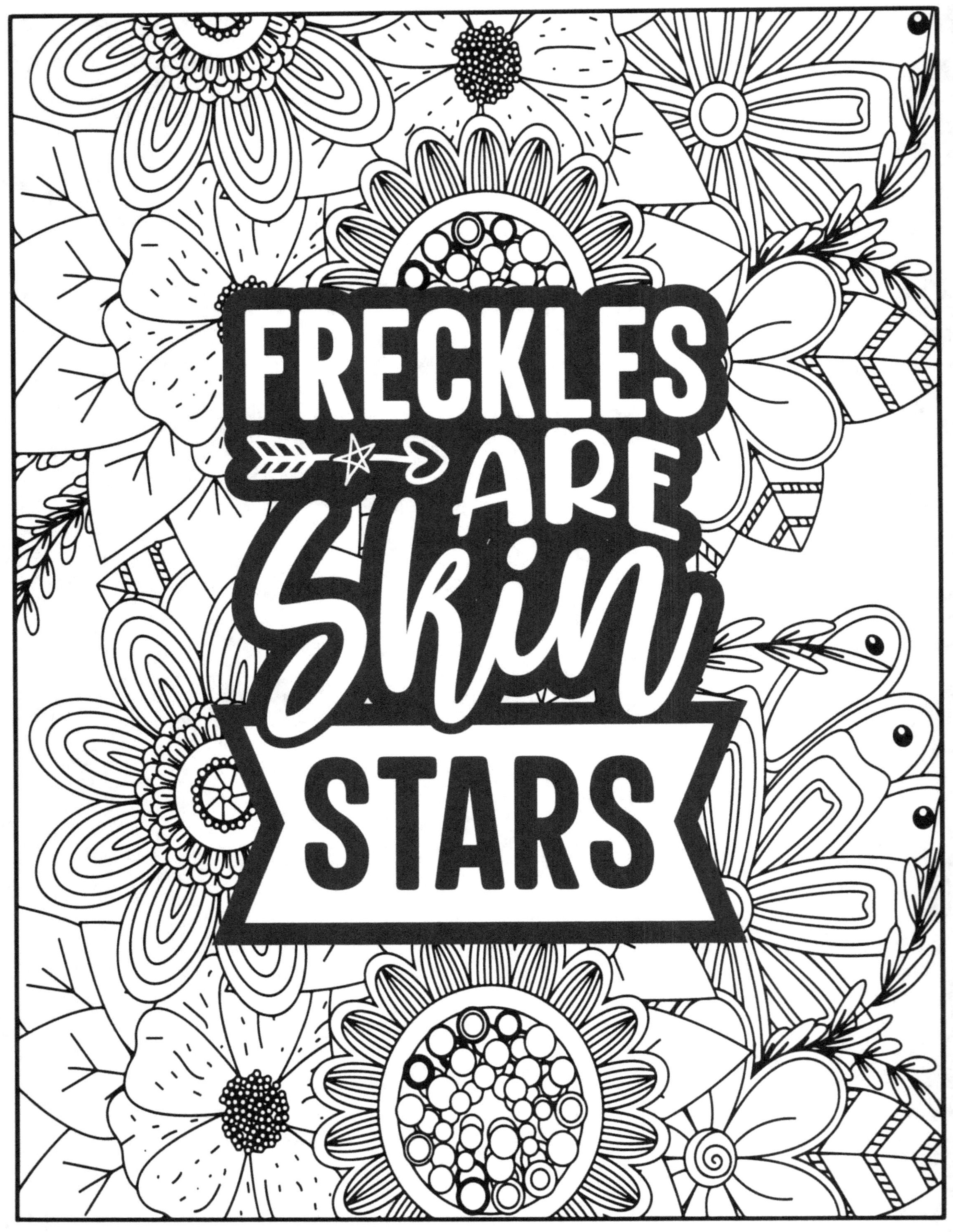

FRECKLES
ARE
Skin
STARS

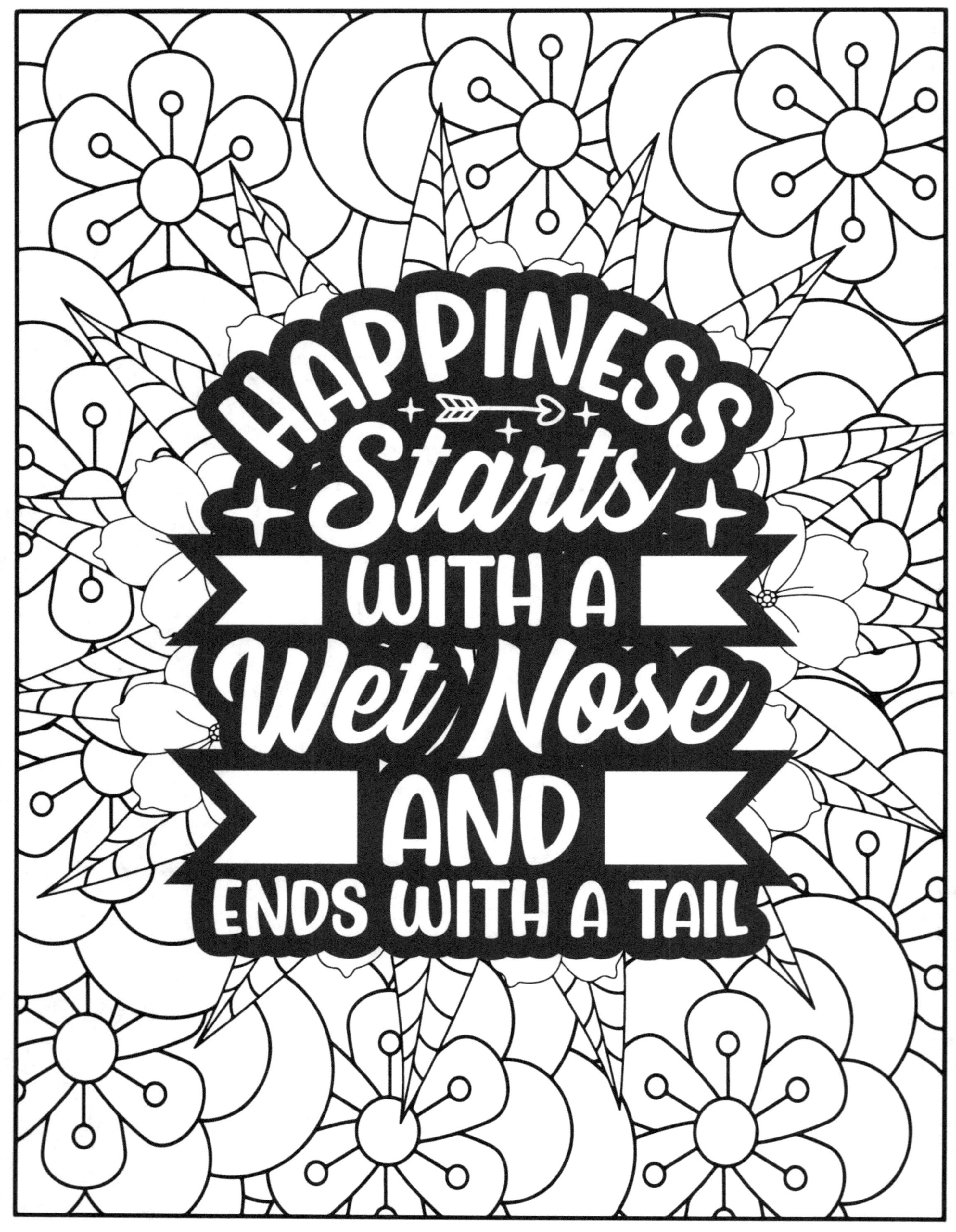

HAPPINESS
Starts
WITH A
Wet Nose
AND
ENDS WITH A TAIL

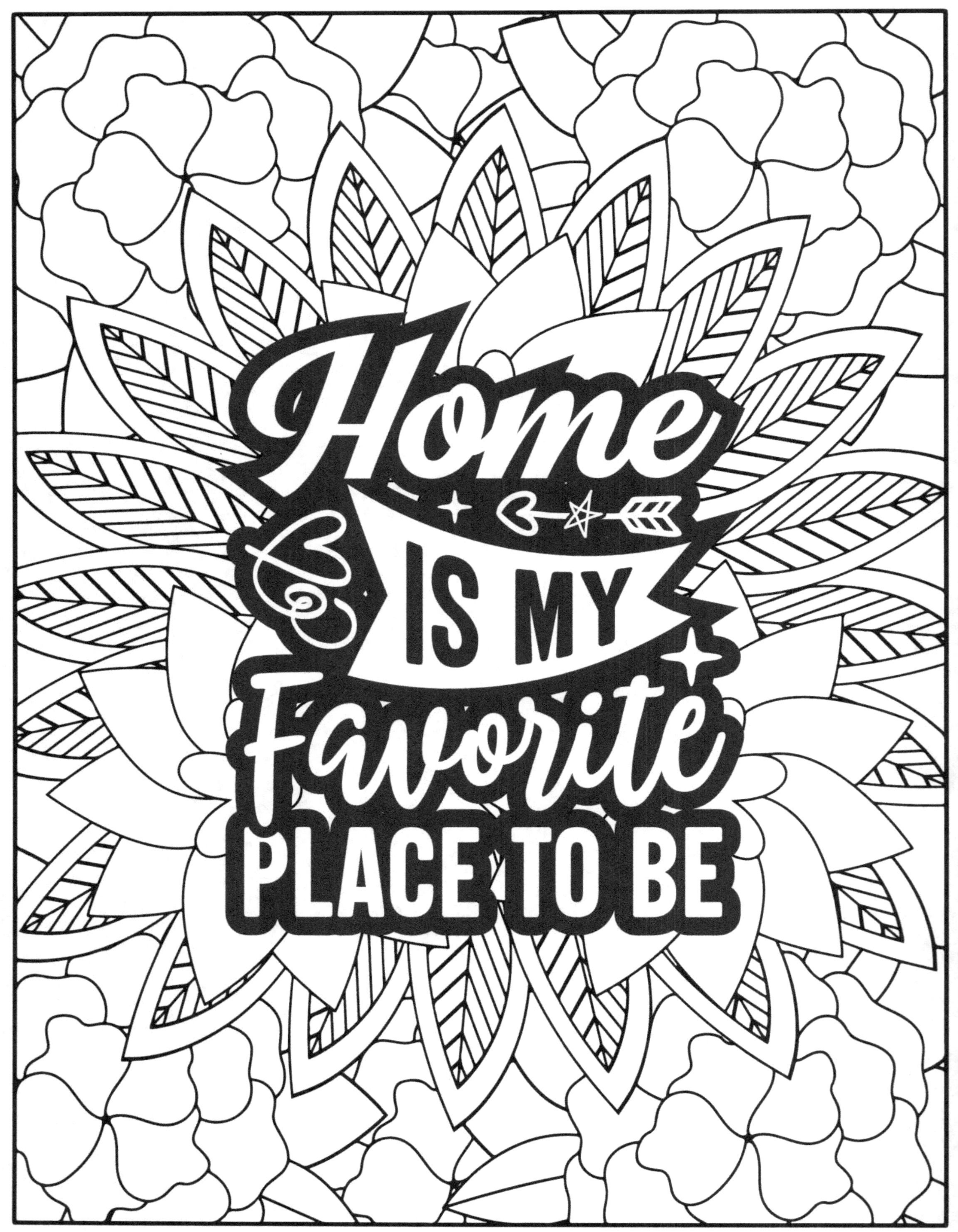
Home
Is my
Favorite
PLACE TO BE

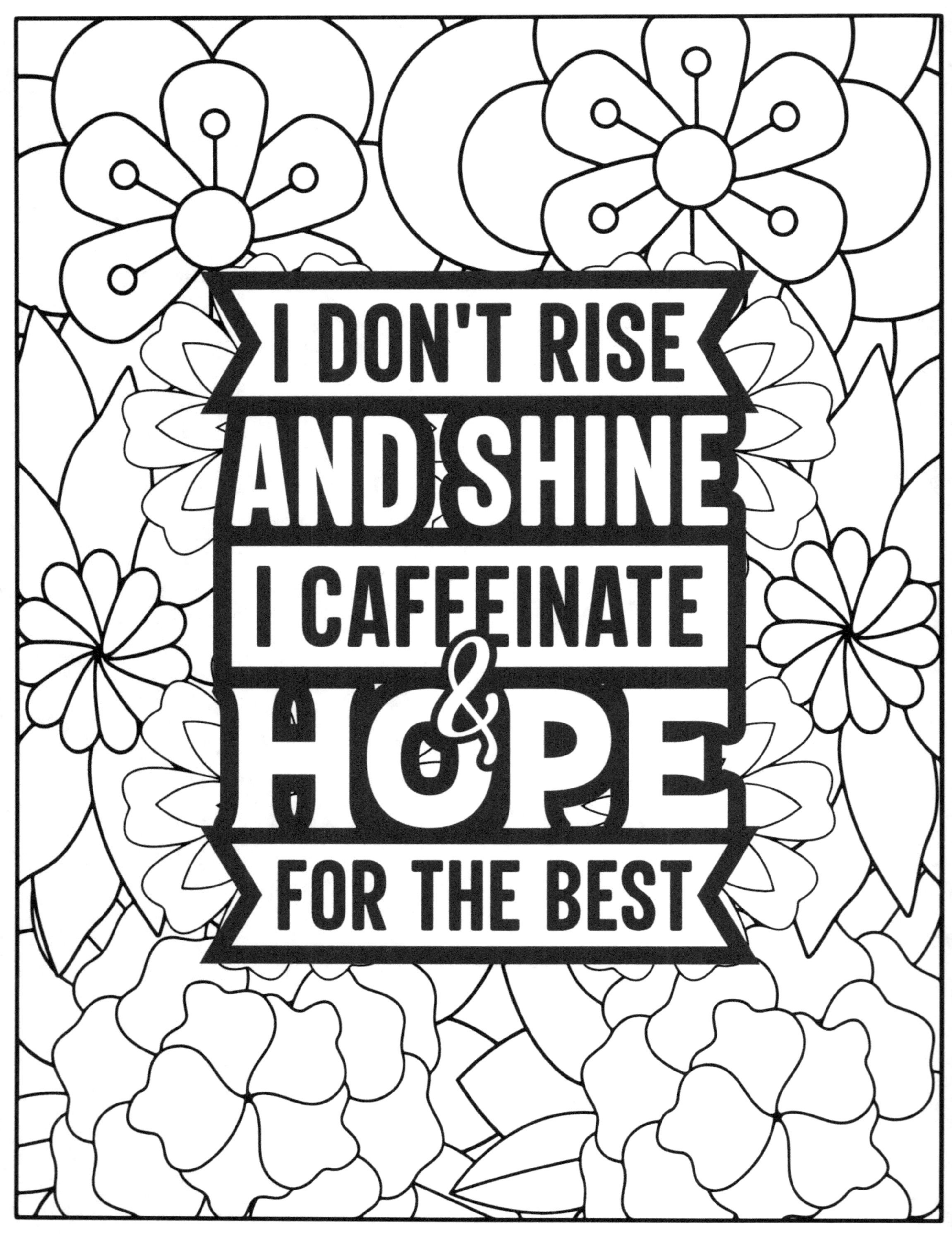

I DON'T RISE
AND SHINE
I CAFFEINATE
& HOPE
FOR THE BEST

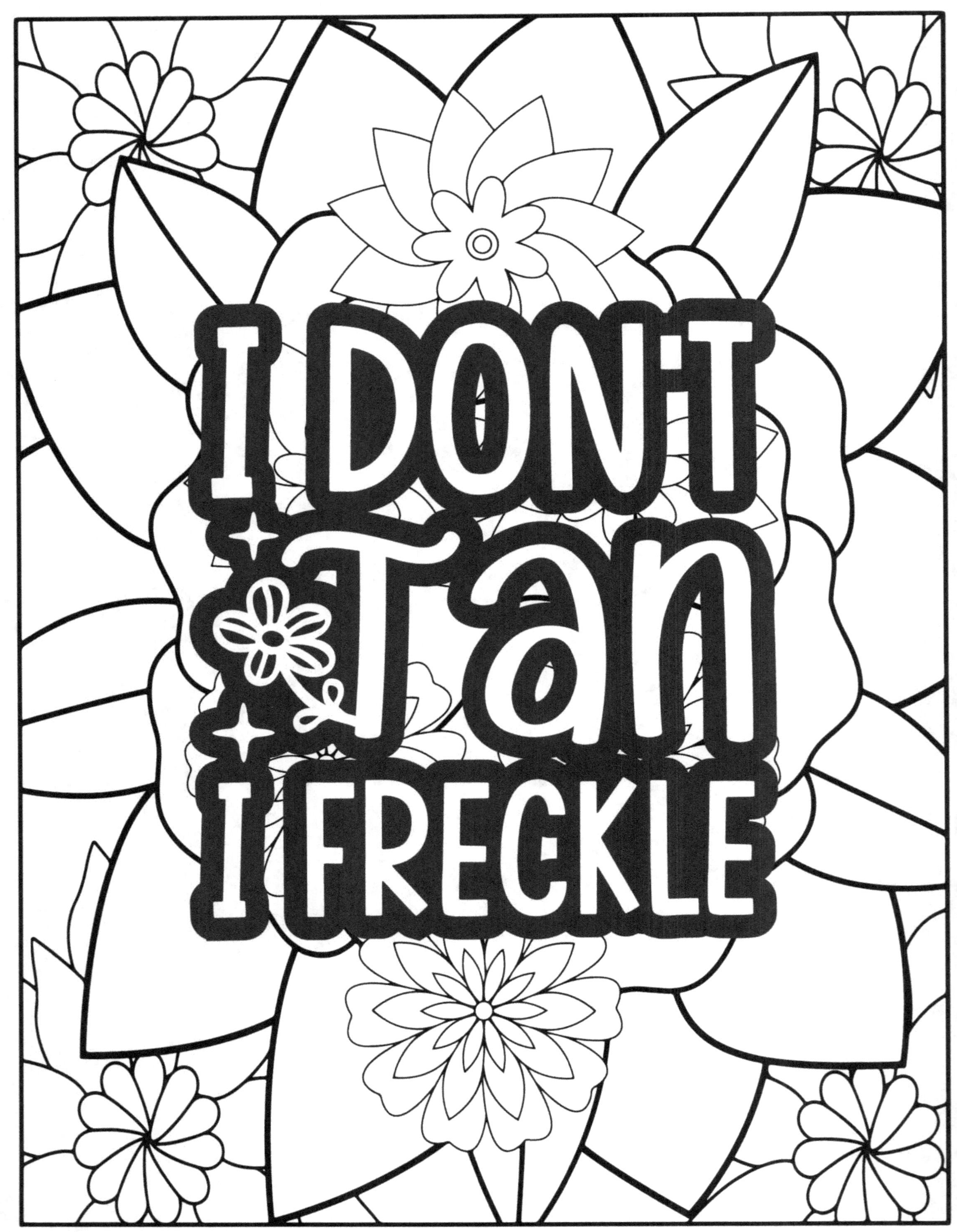

I DON'T
Tan
I FRECKLE

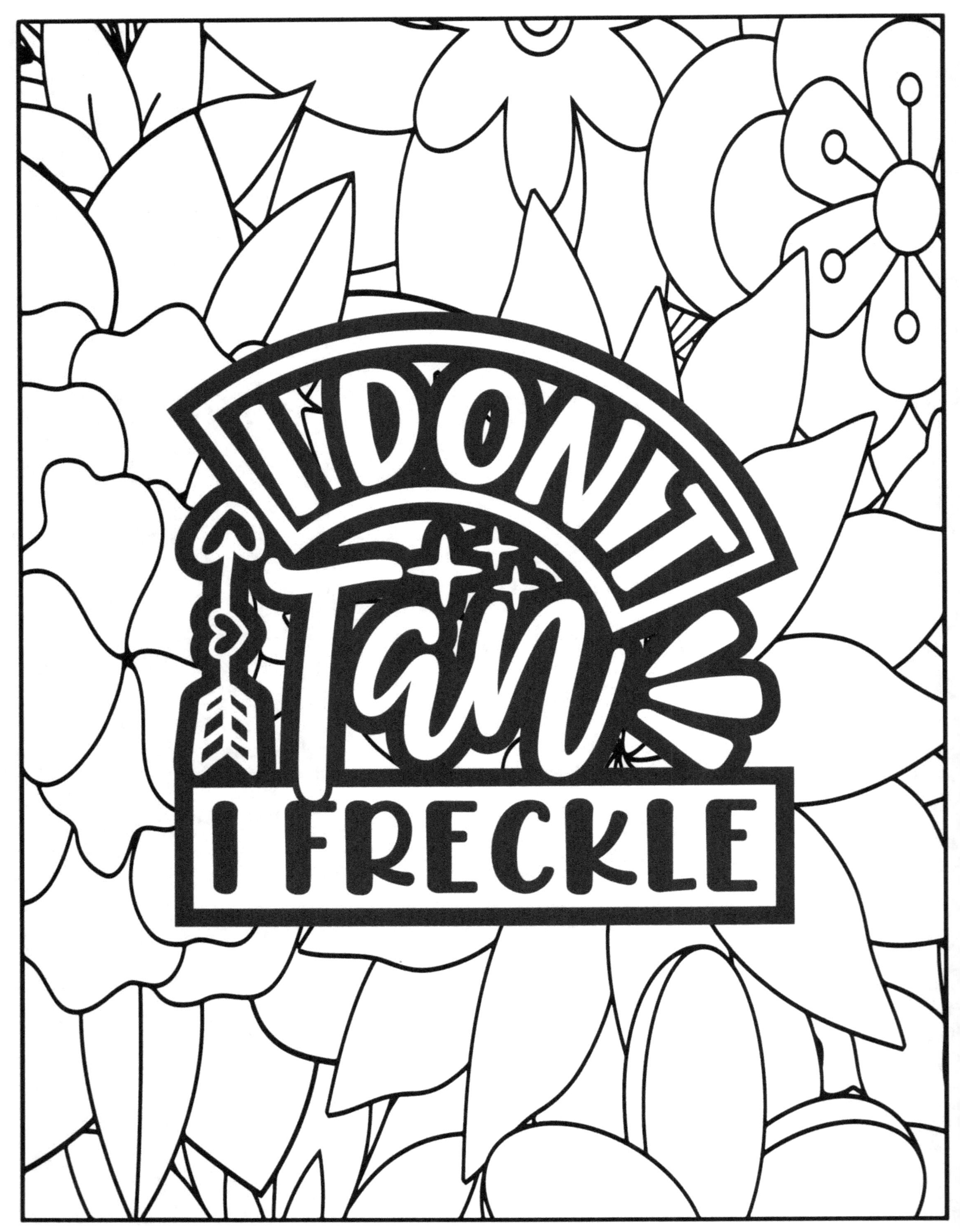

I DON'T
Tan
I FRECKLE

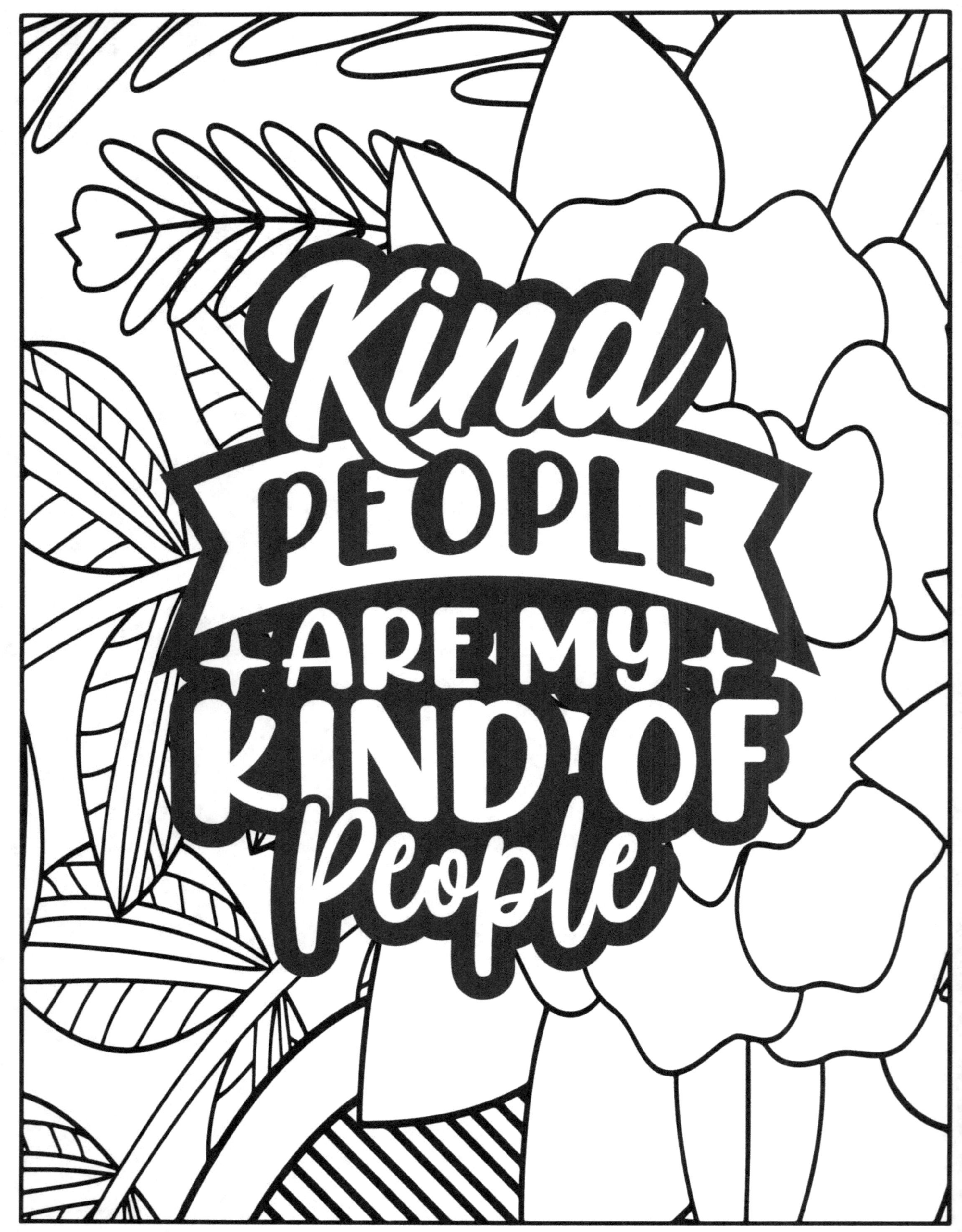

Kind
PEOPLE
ARE MY
KIND OF
People

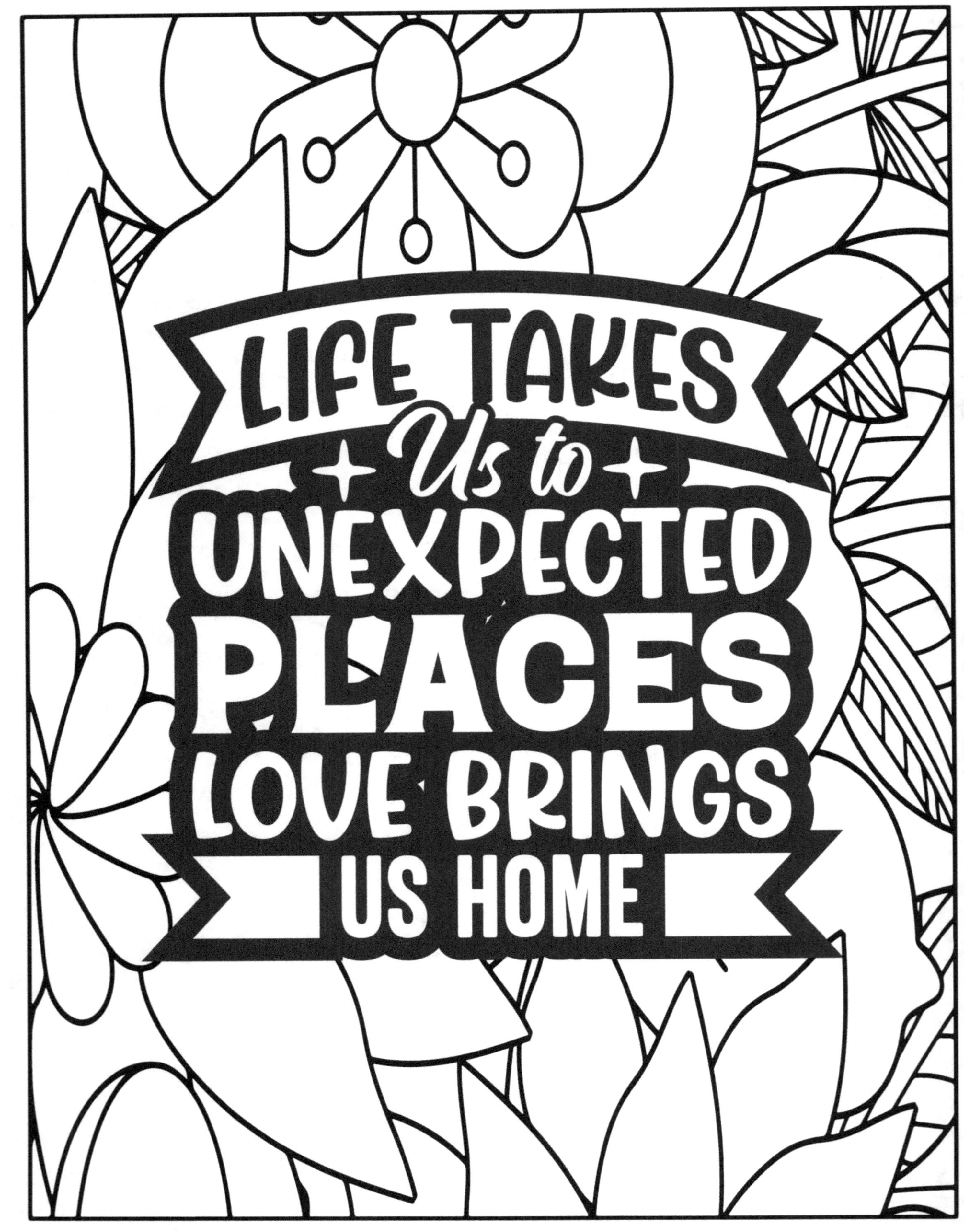

LIFE TAKES
Us to
UNEXPECTED
PLACES
LOVE BRINGS
US HOME

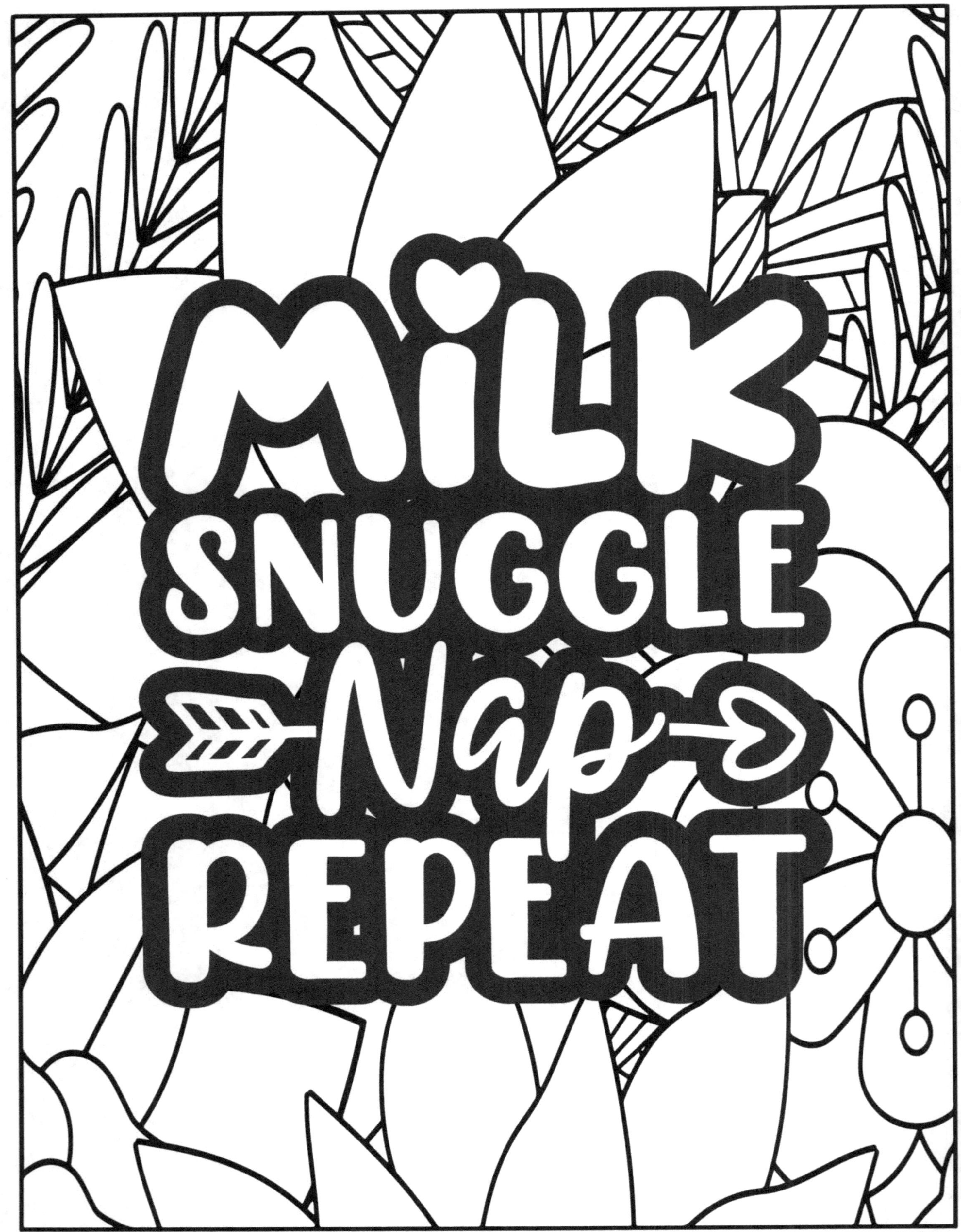

Milk
SNUGGLE
Nap
REPEAT

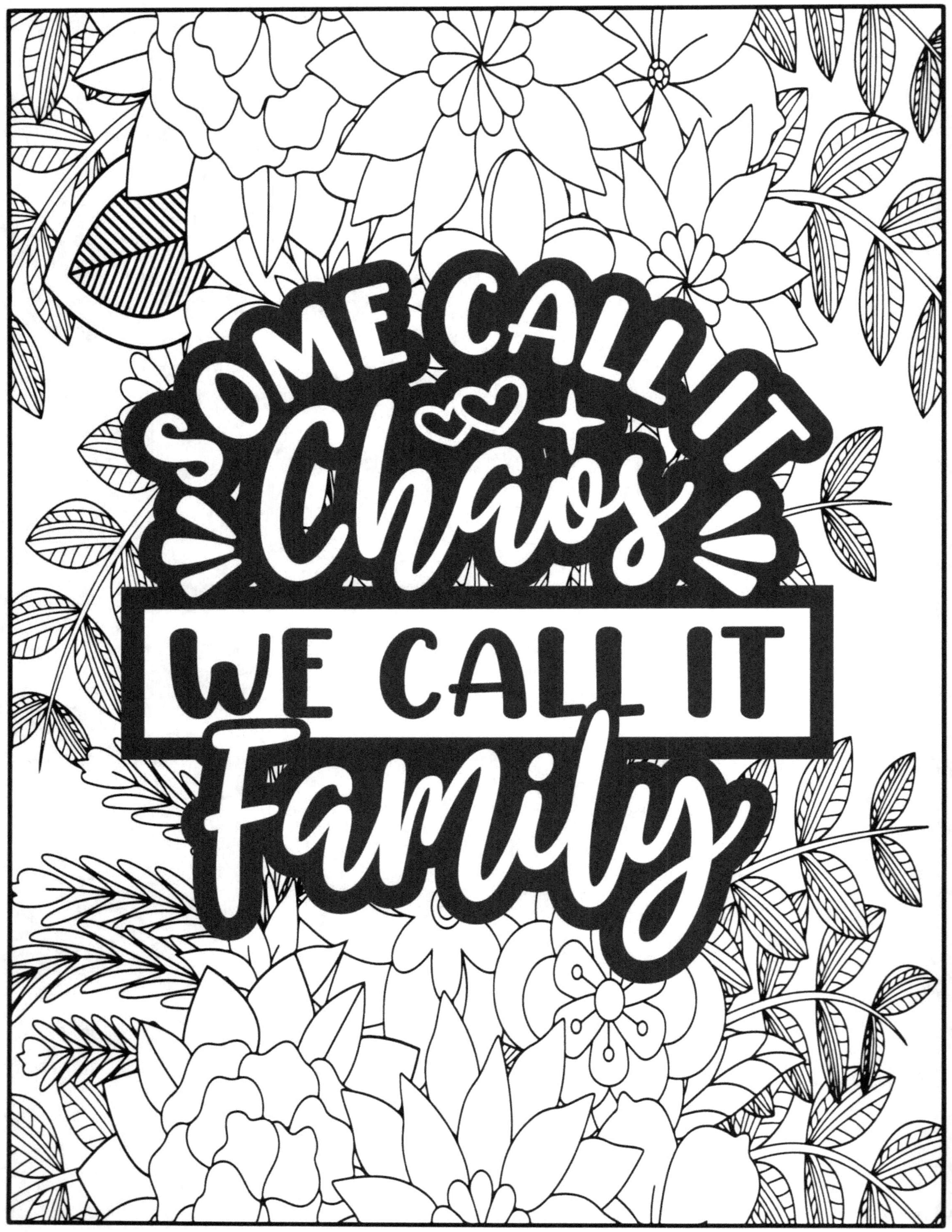

SOME CALL IT
Chaos
WE CALL IT
Family

THE DINING ROOM

WHERE Friends BECOME FAMILY

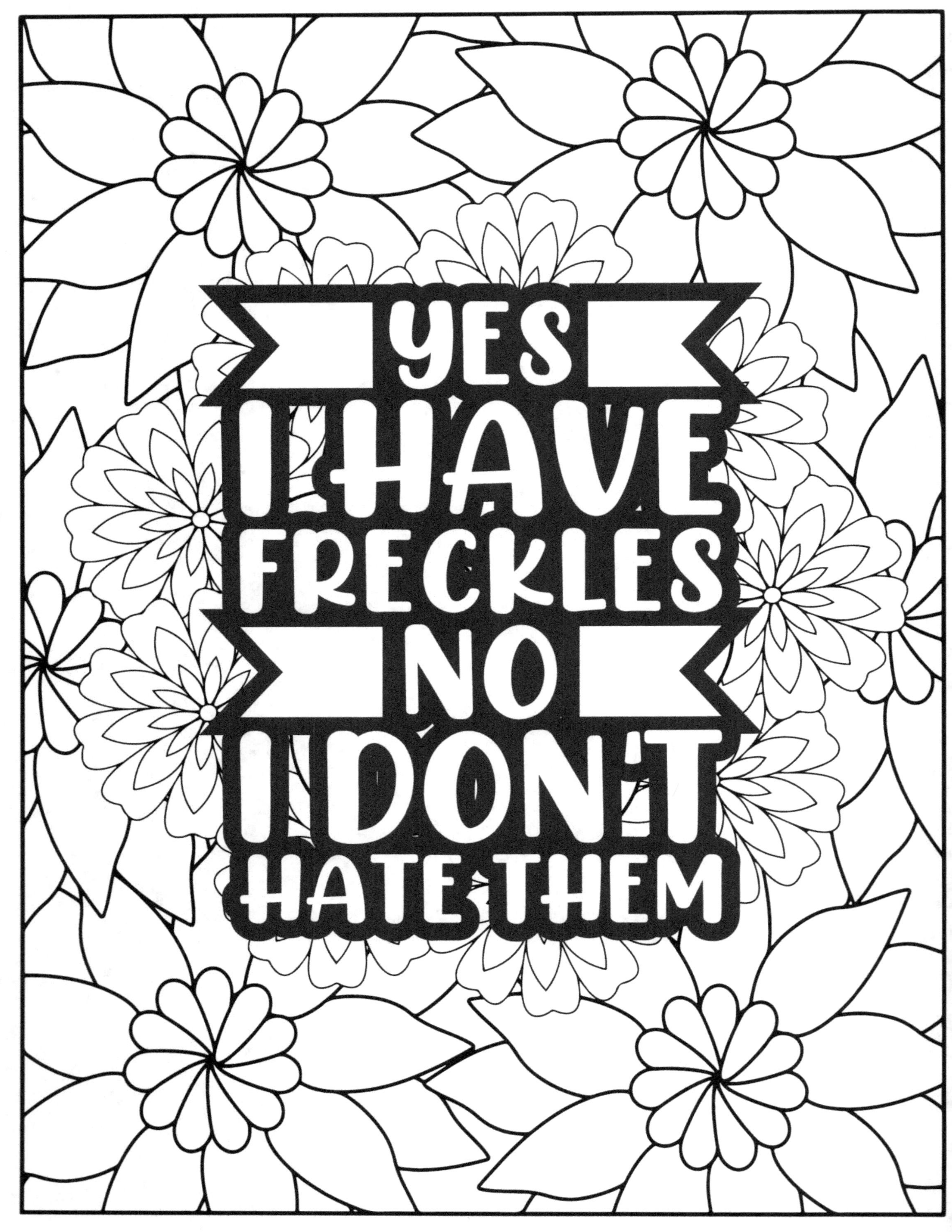

YES
I HAVE
FRECKLES
NO
I DON'T
HATE THEM

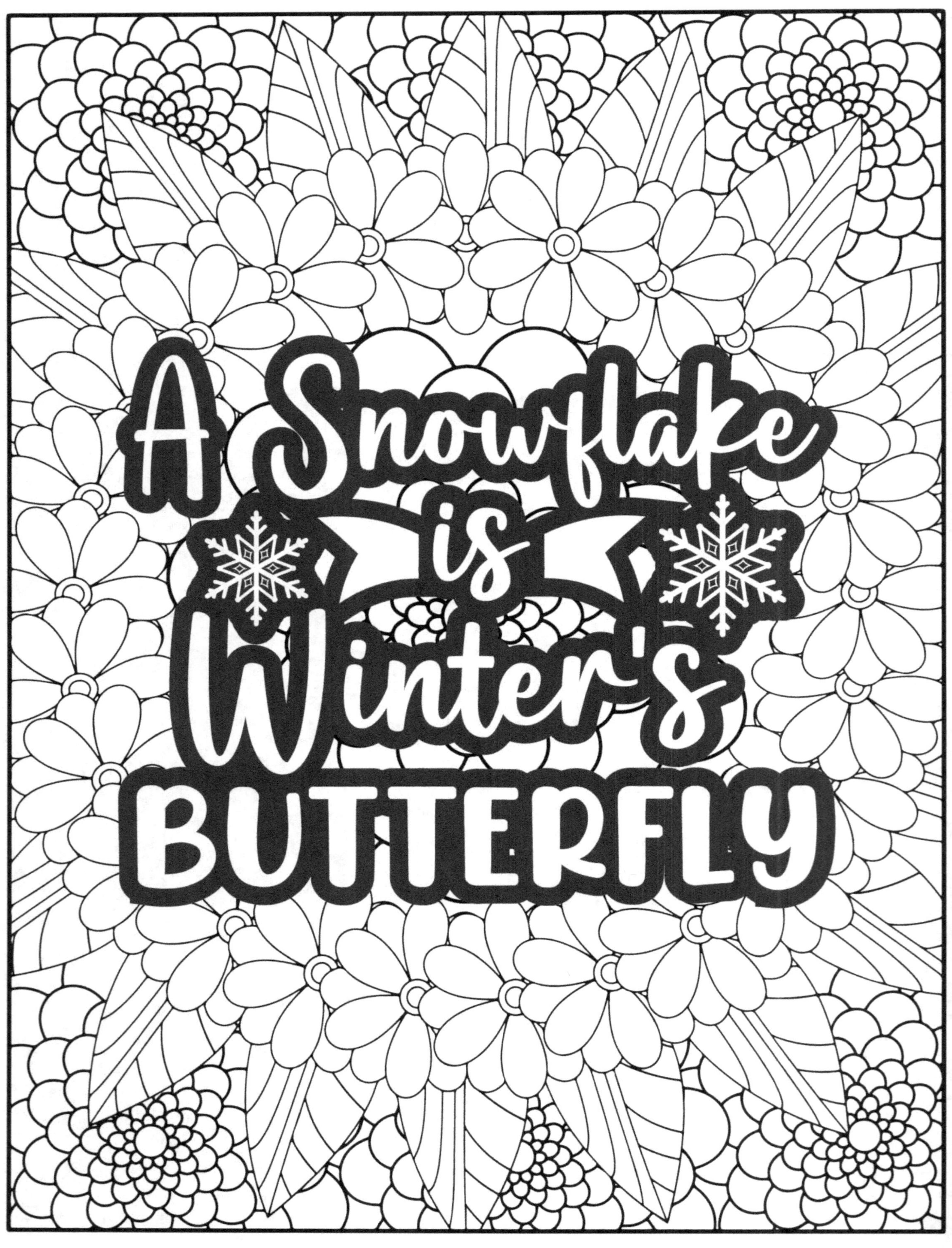

A Snowflake
is
Winter's
BUTTERFLY

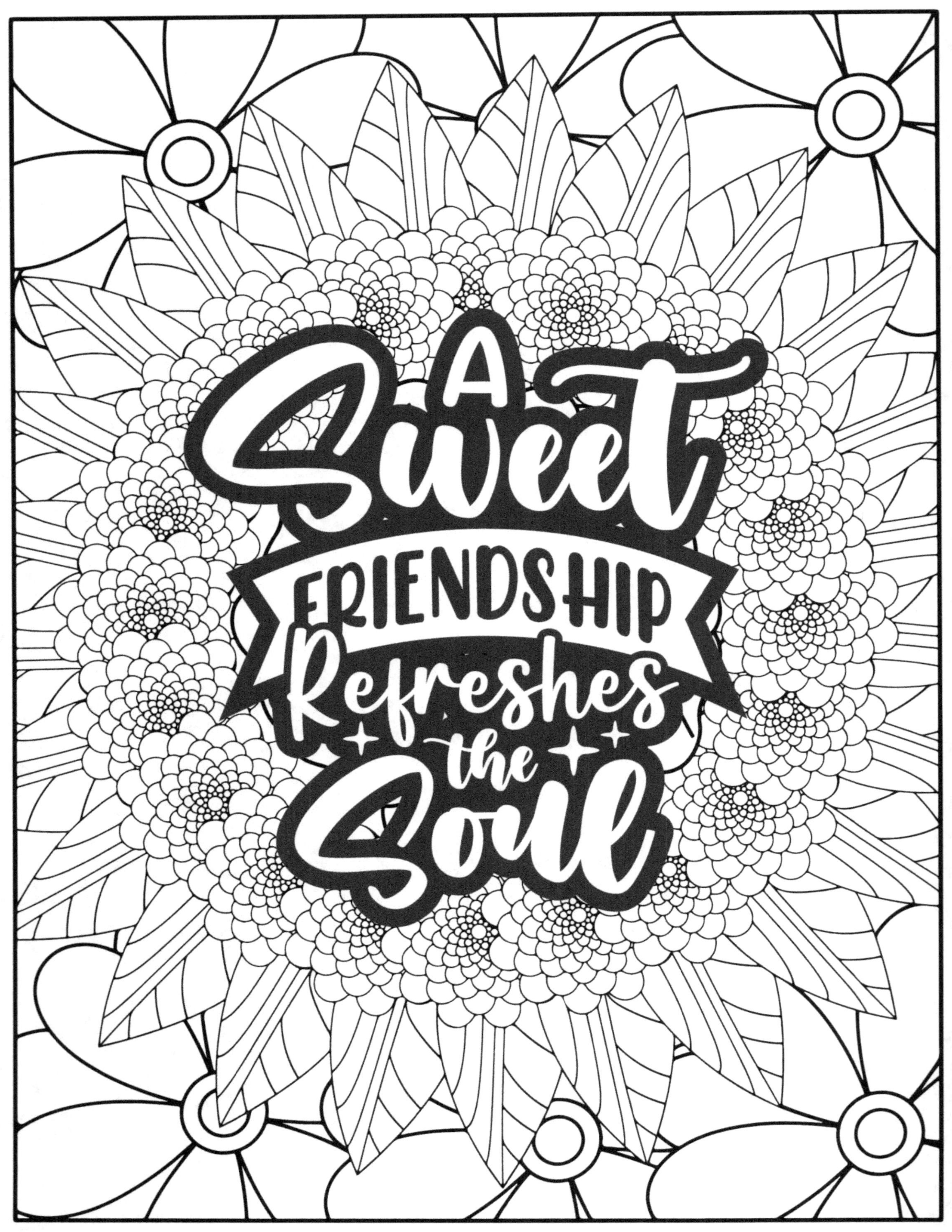

A Sweet
FRIENDSHIP
Refreshes
the
Soul

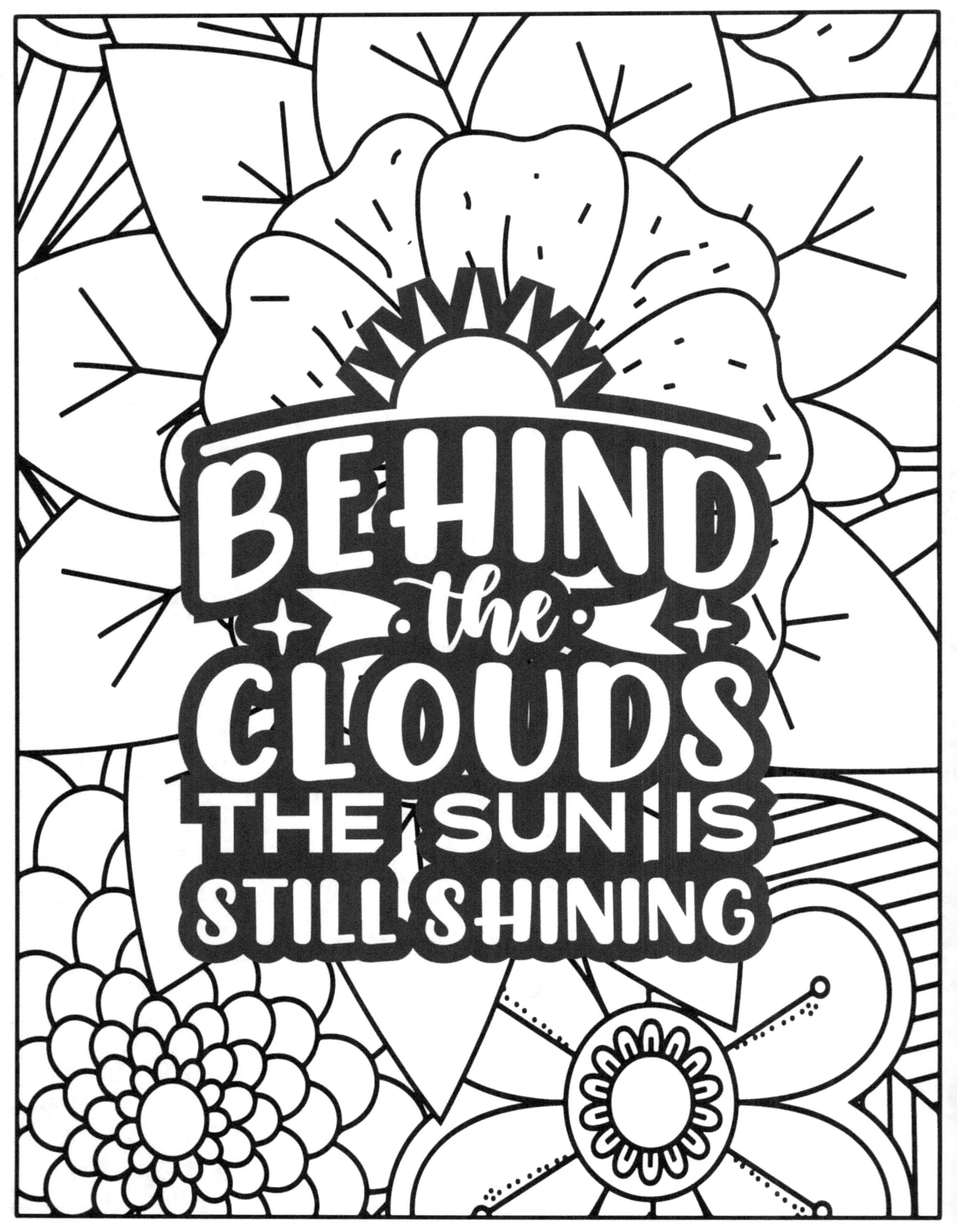

BEHIND
the
CLOUDS
THE SUN IS
STILL SHINING

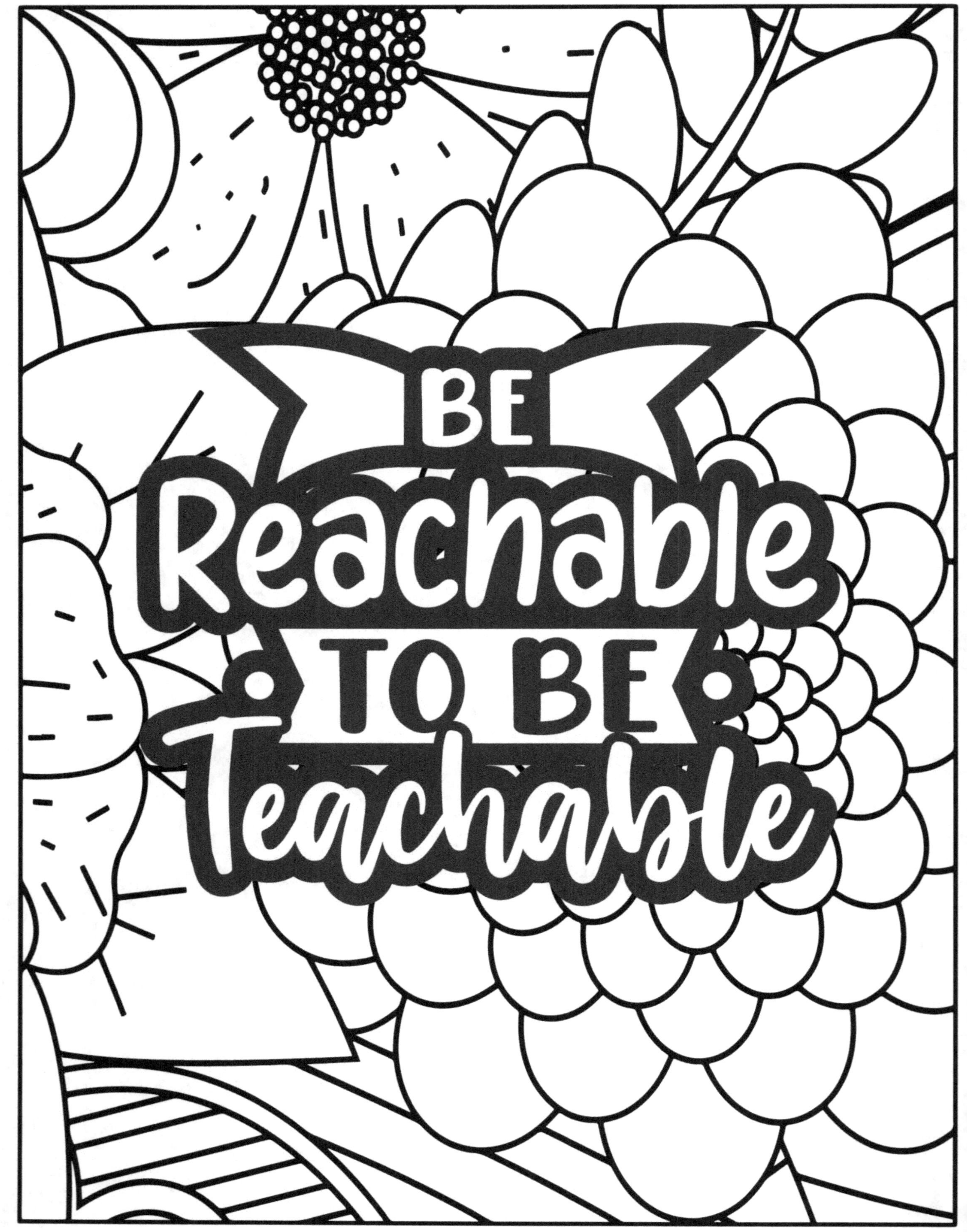

BE
Reachable
TO BE
Teachable

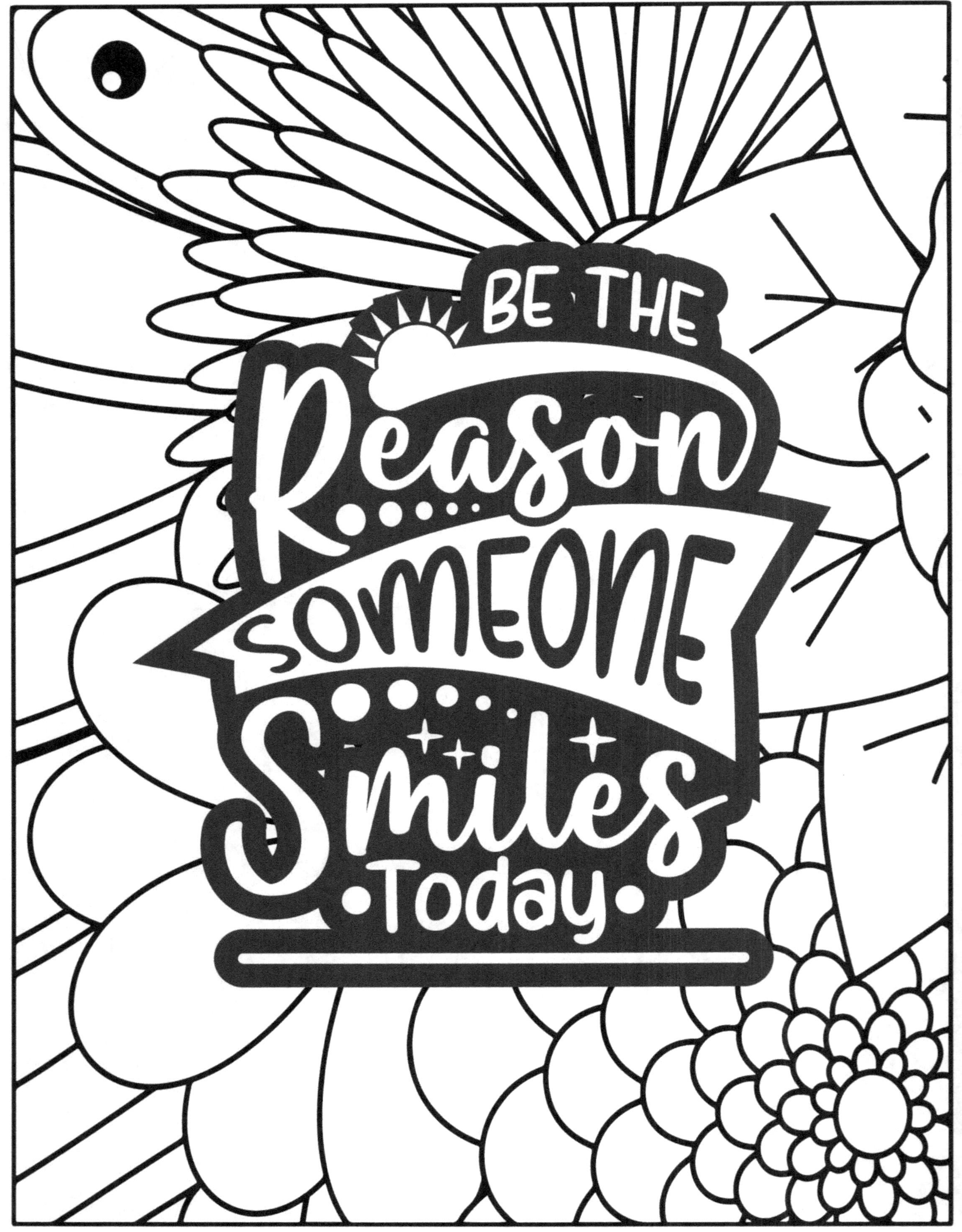

BE THE
Reason
SOMEONE
Smiles
Today

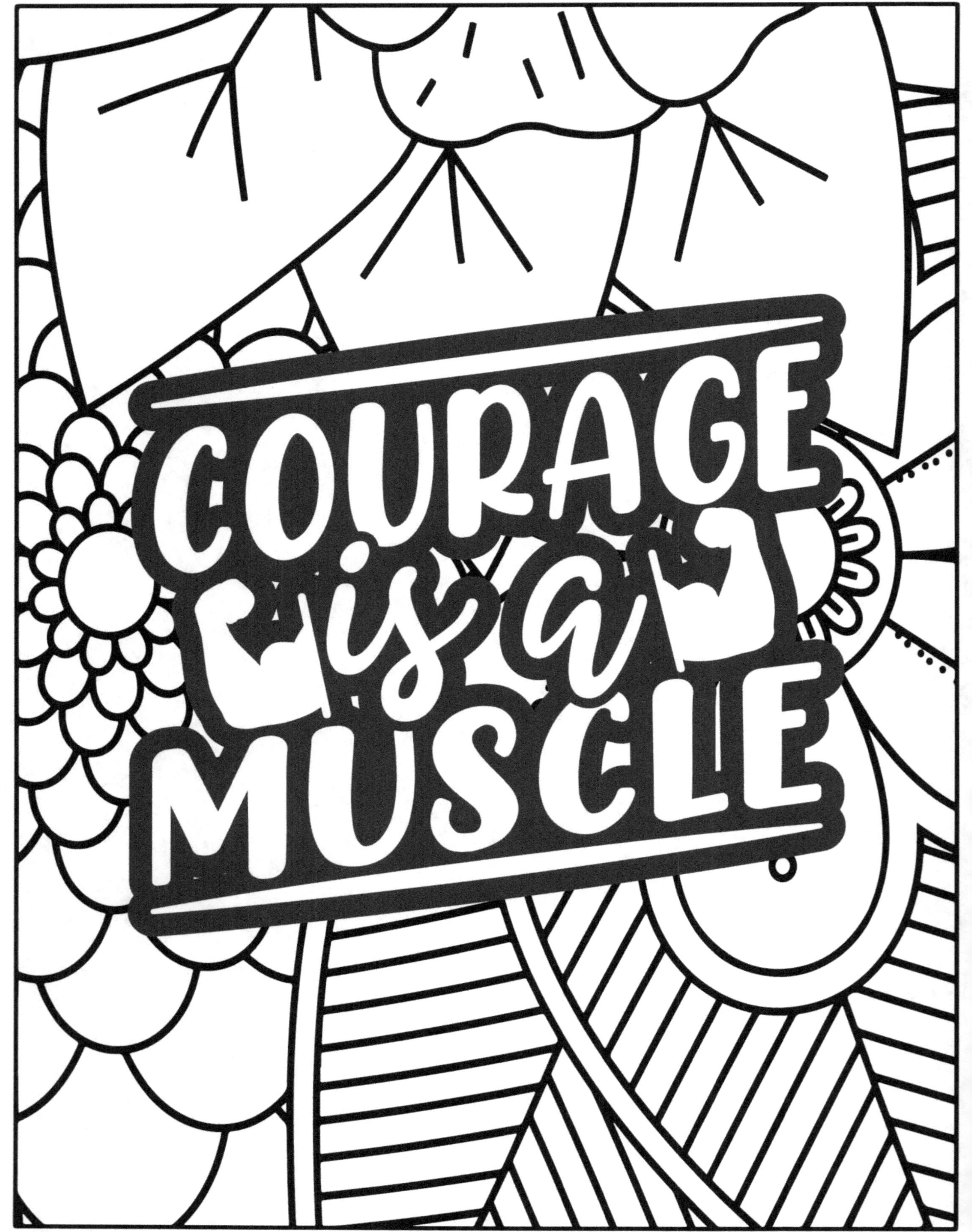

COURAGE
is a
MUSCLE

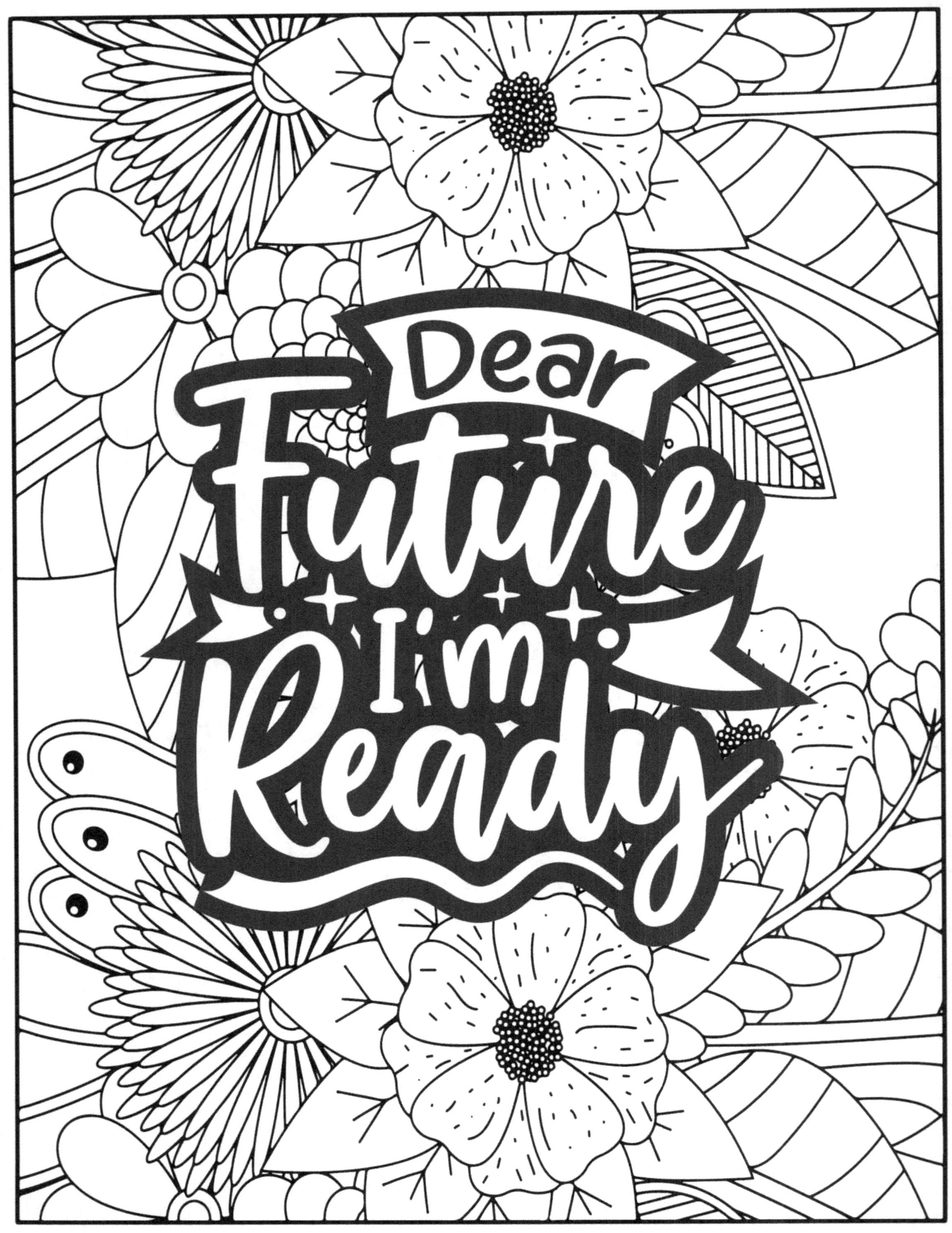

Dear
Future
I'm
Ready

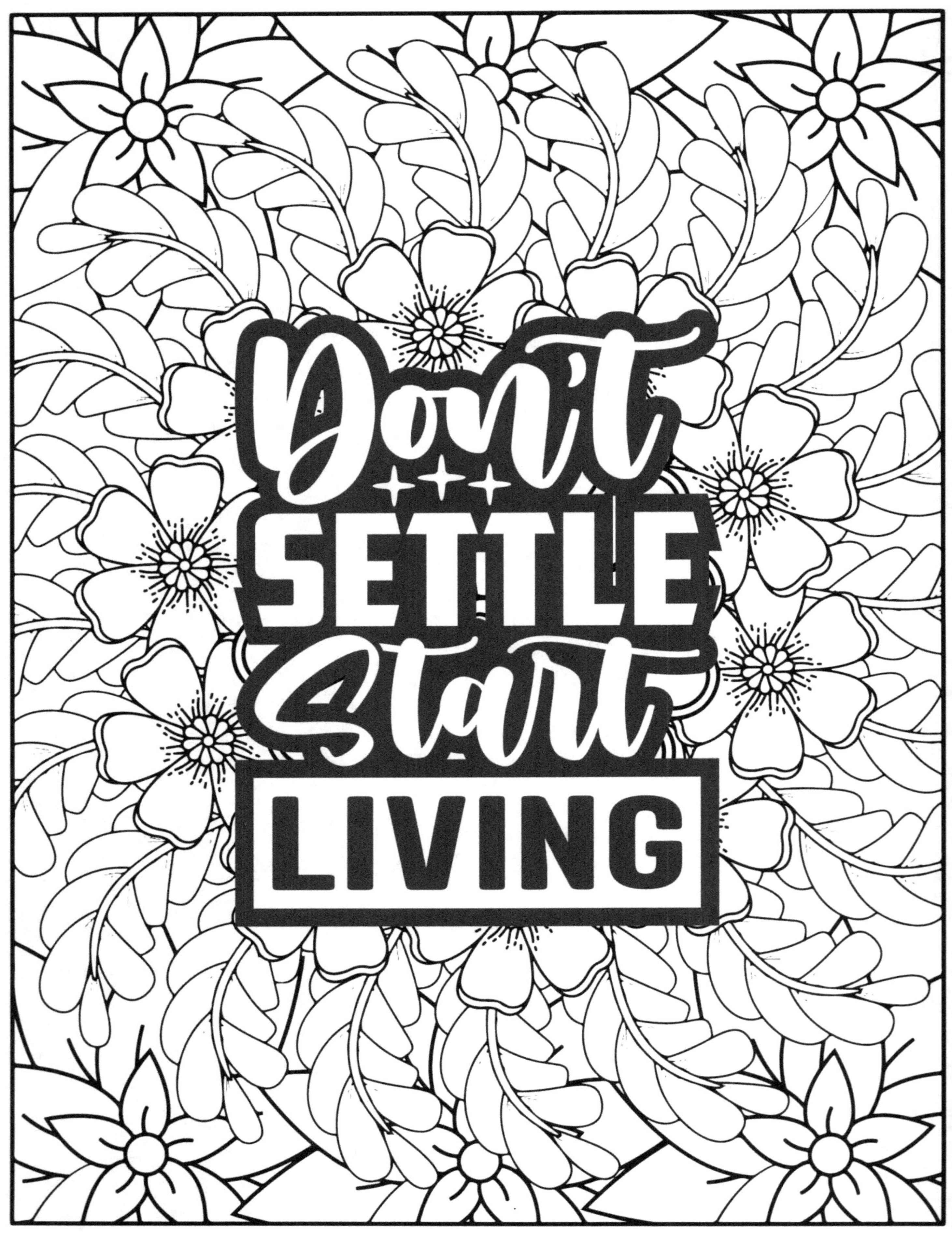

Don't
SETTLE
Start
LIVING

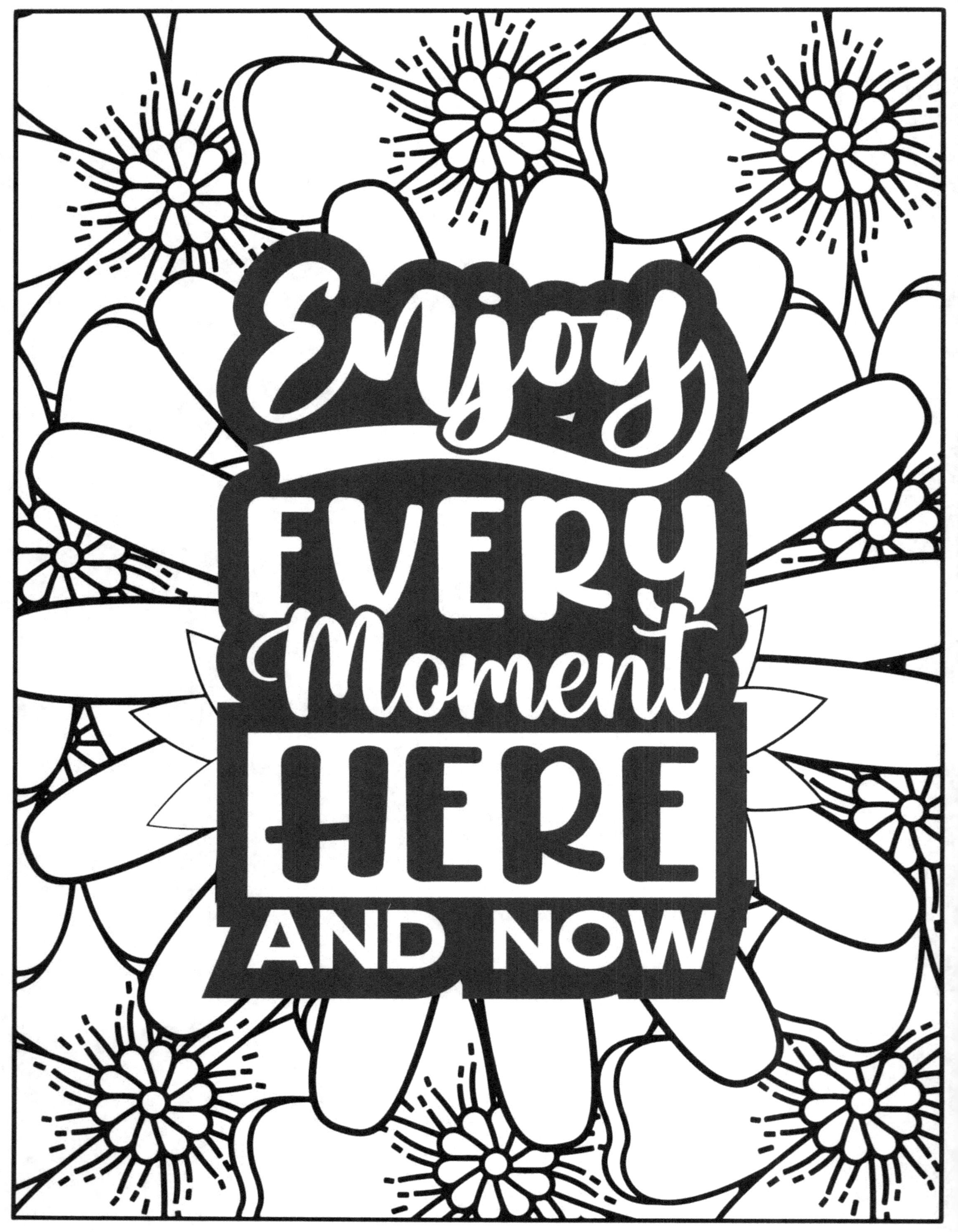

Enjoy
EVERY
Moment
HERE
AND NOW

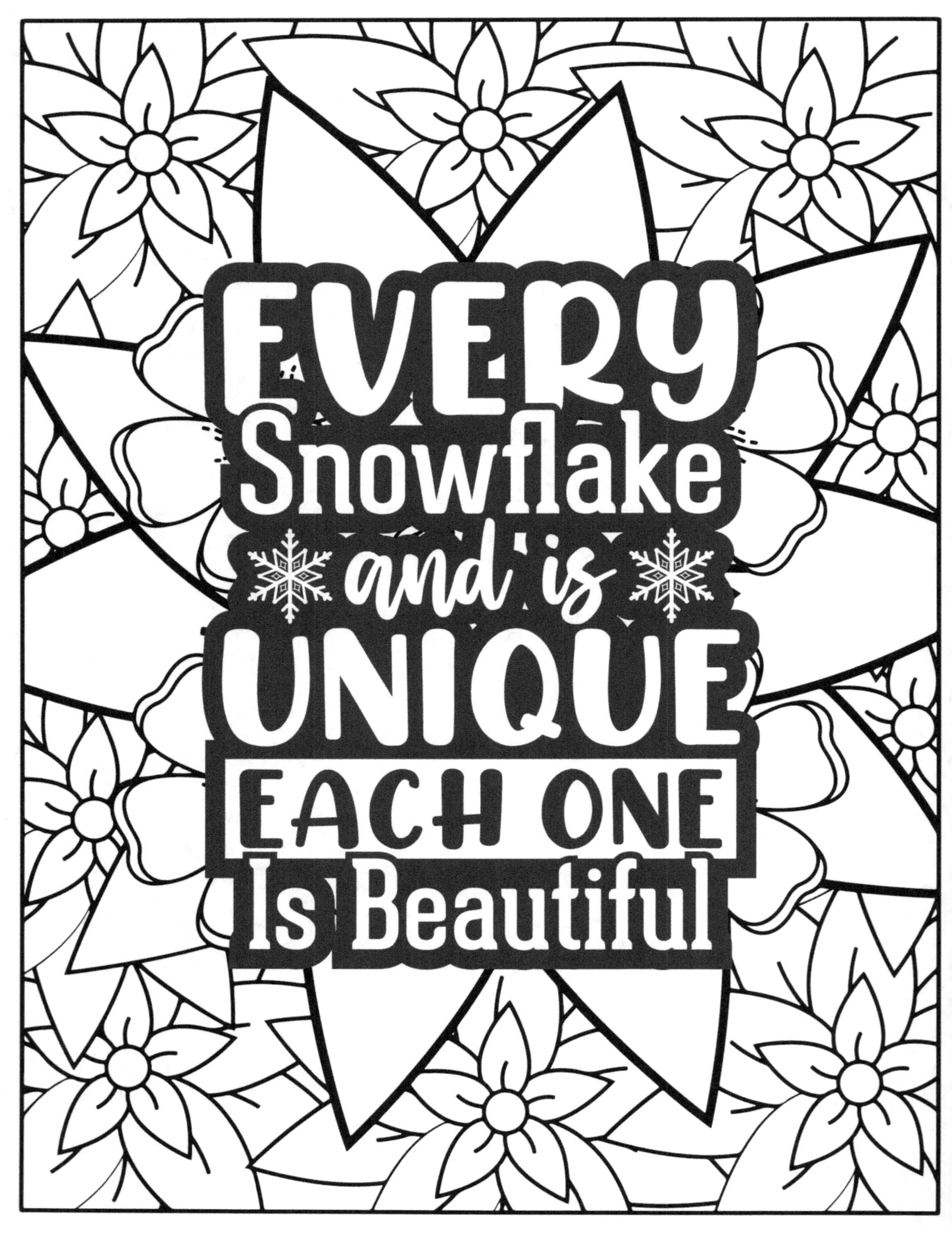

EVERY
Snowflake
and is
UNIQUE
EACH ONE
Is Beautiful

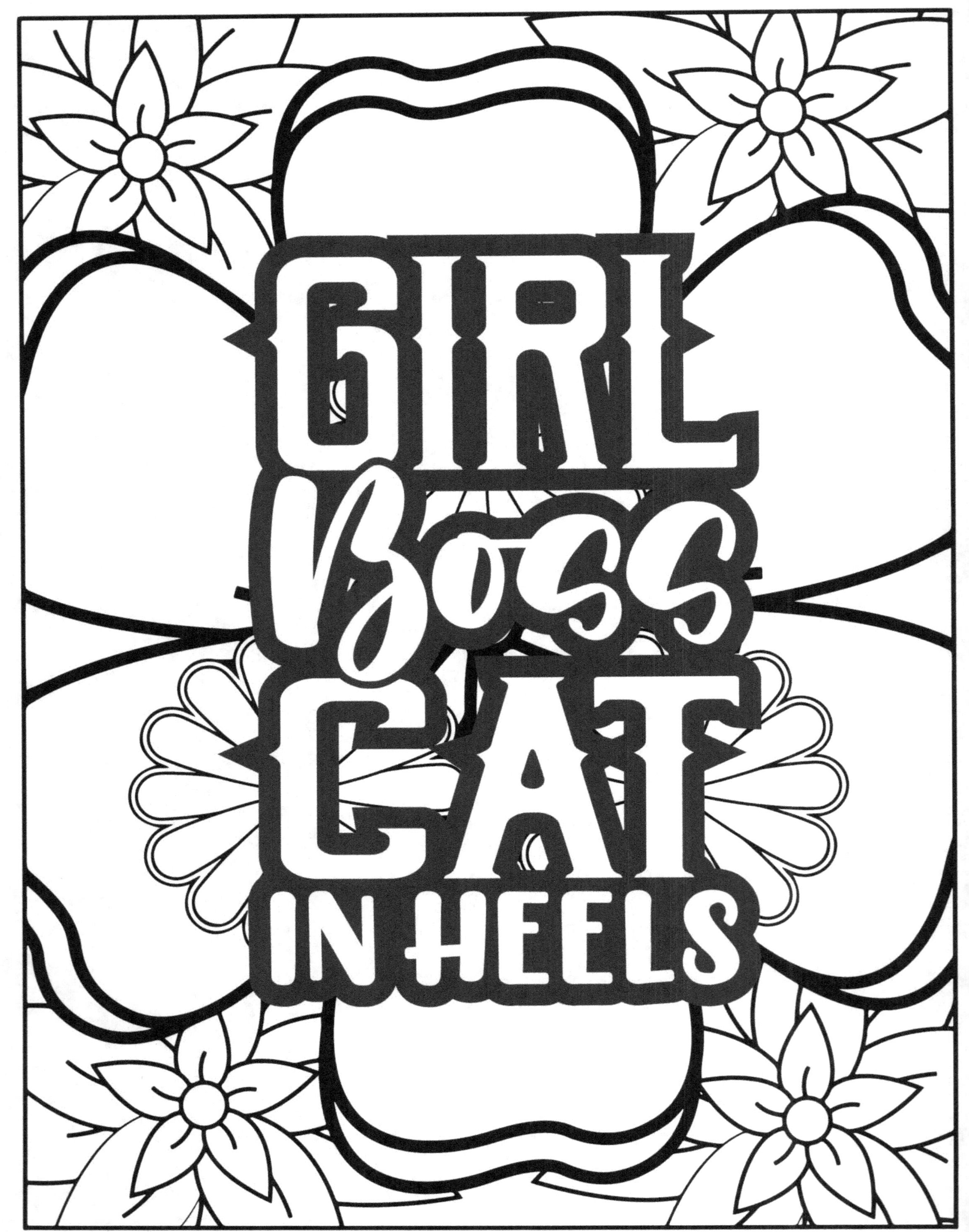

GIRL
BOSS
CAT
IN HEELS

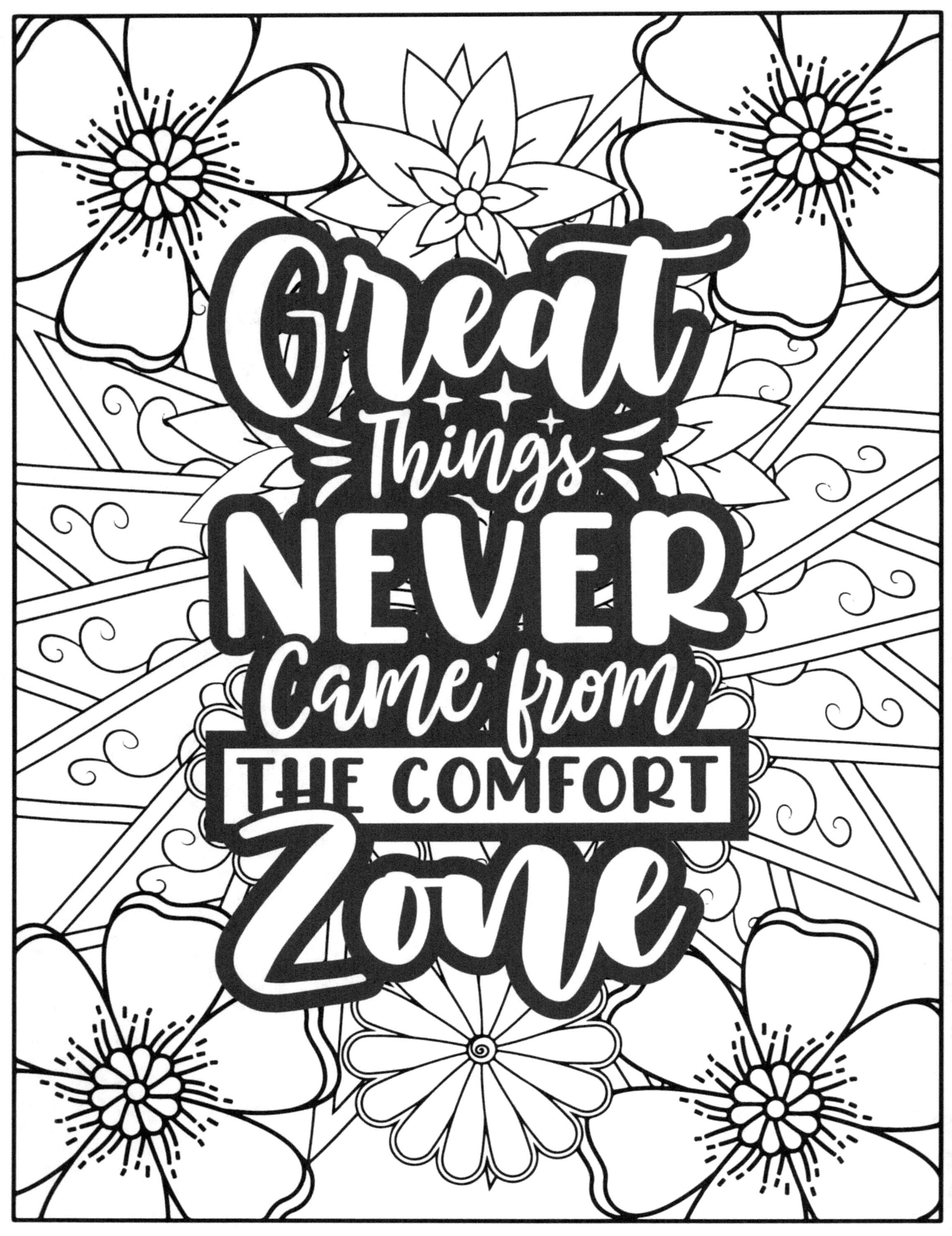

Great
Things
NEVER
Came from
THE COMFORT
Zone

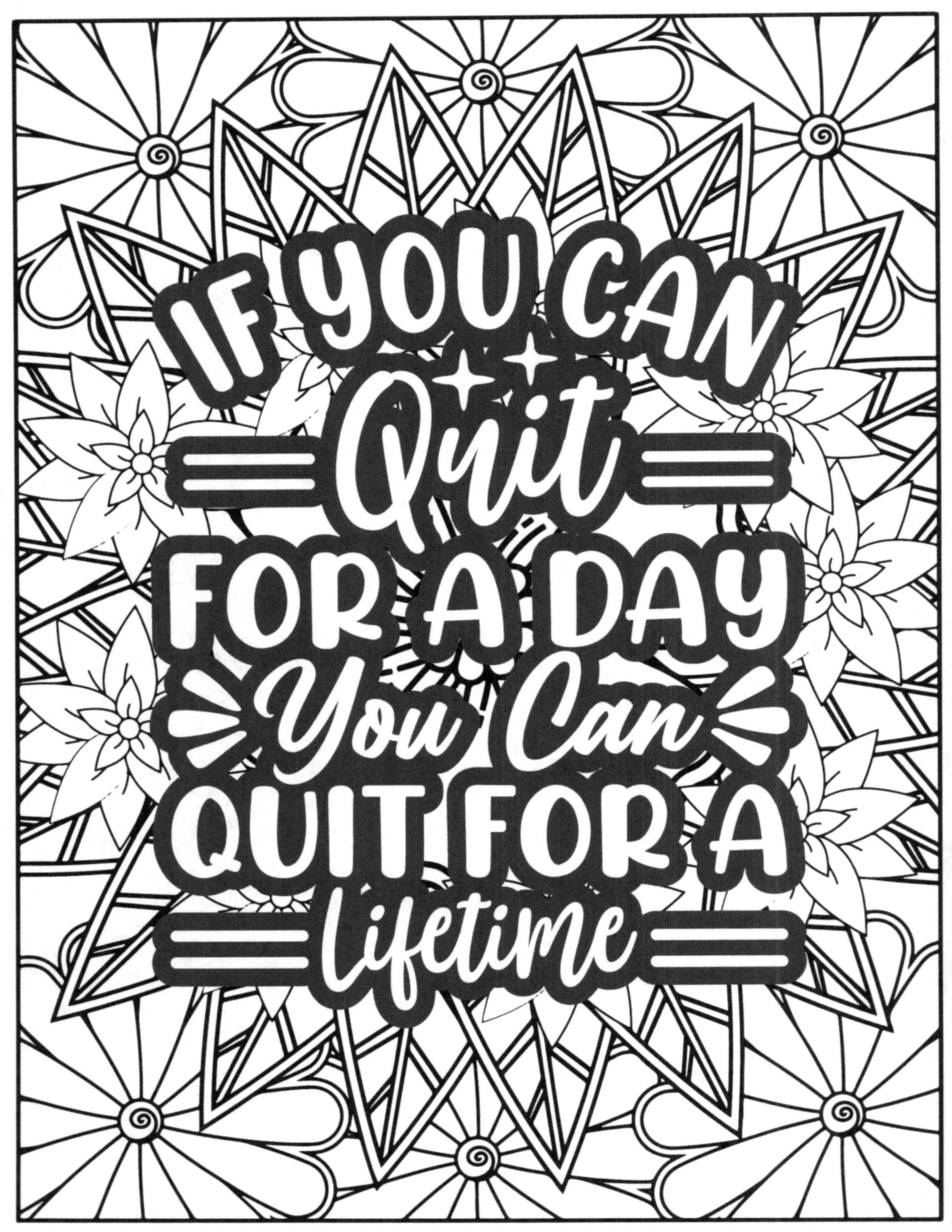

IF YOU CAN
Quit
FOR A DAY
You Can
QUIT FOR A
lifetime

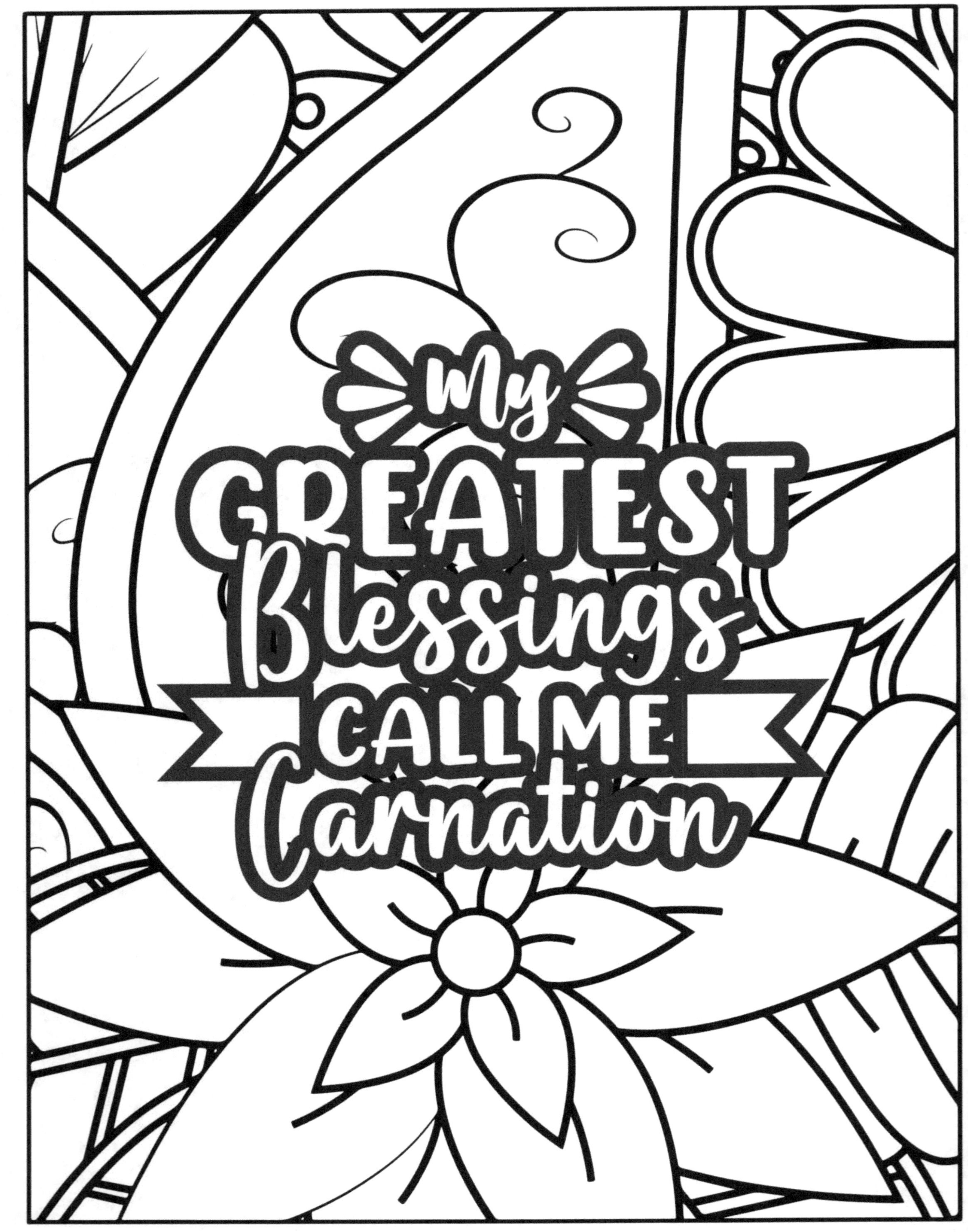

My
GREATEST
Blessings
CALL ME
Carnation

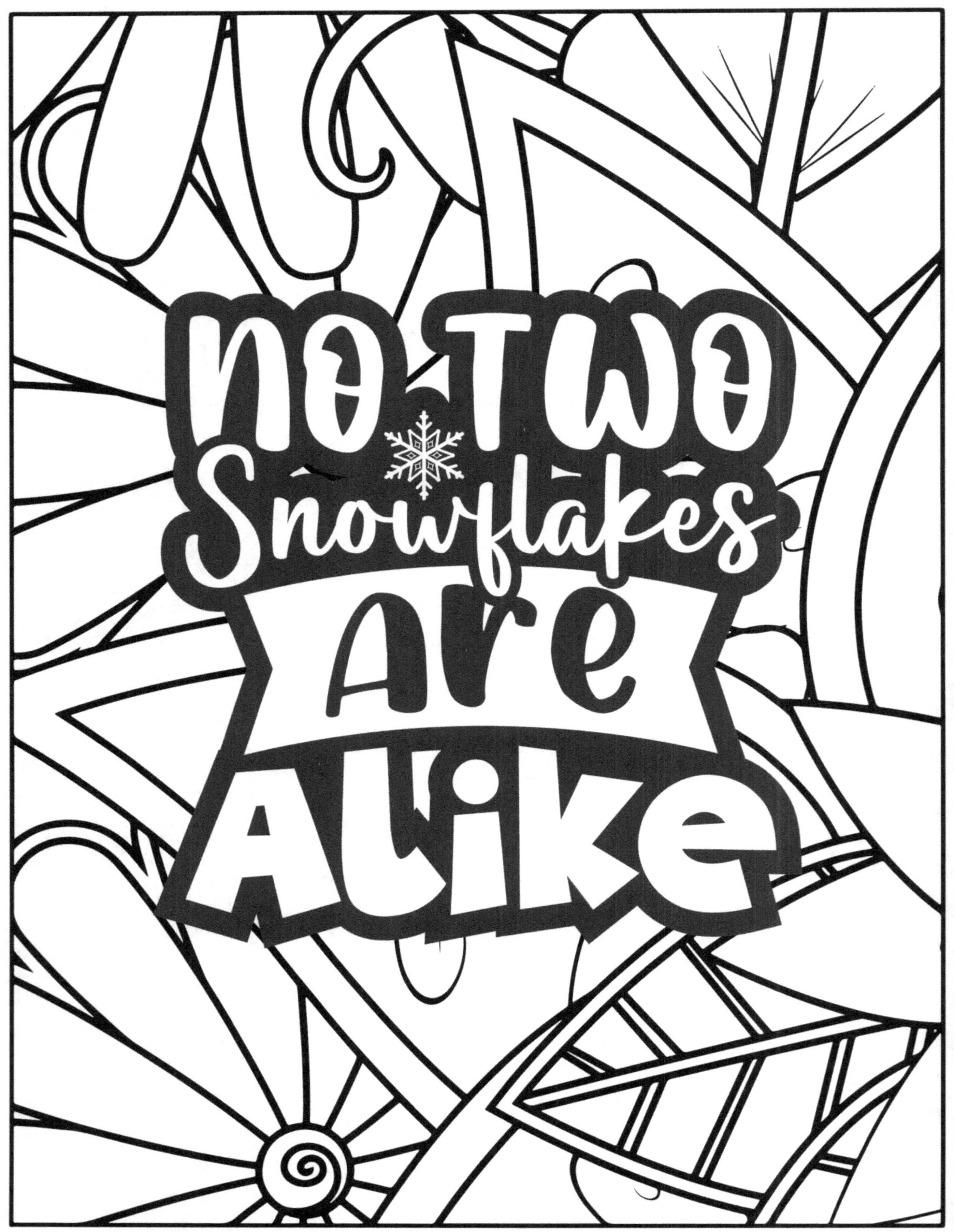

NO TWO
Snowflakes
Are
Alike

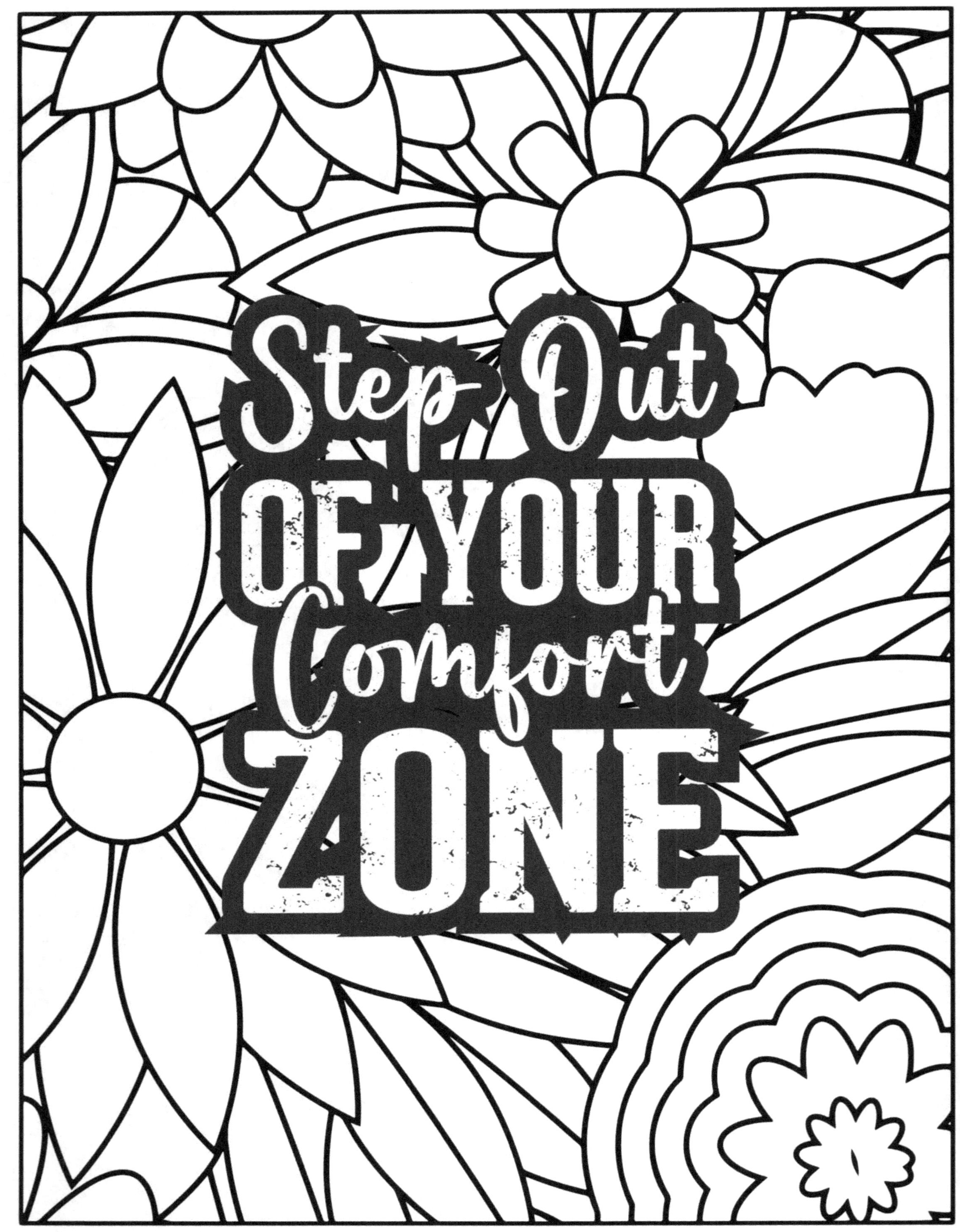

Step Out
OF YOUR
Comfort
ZONE

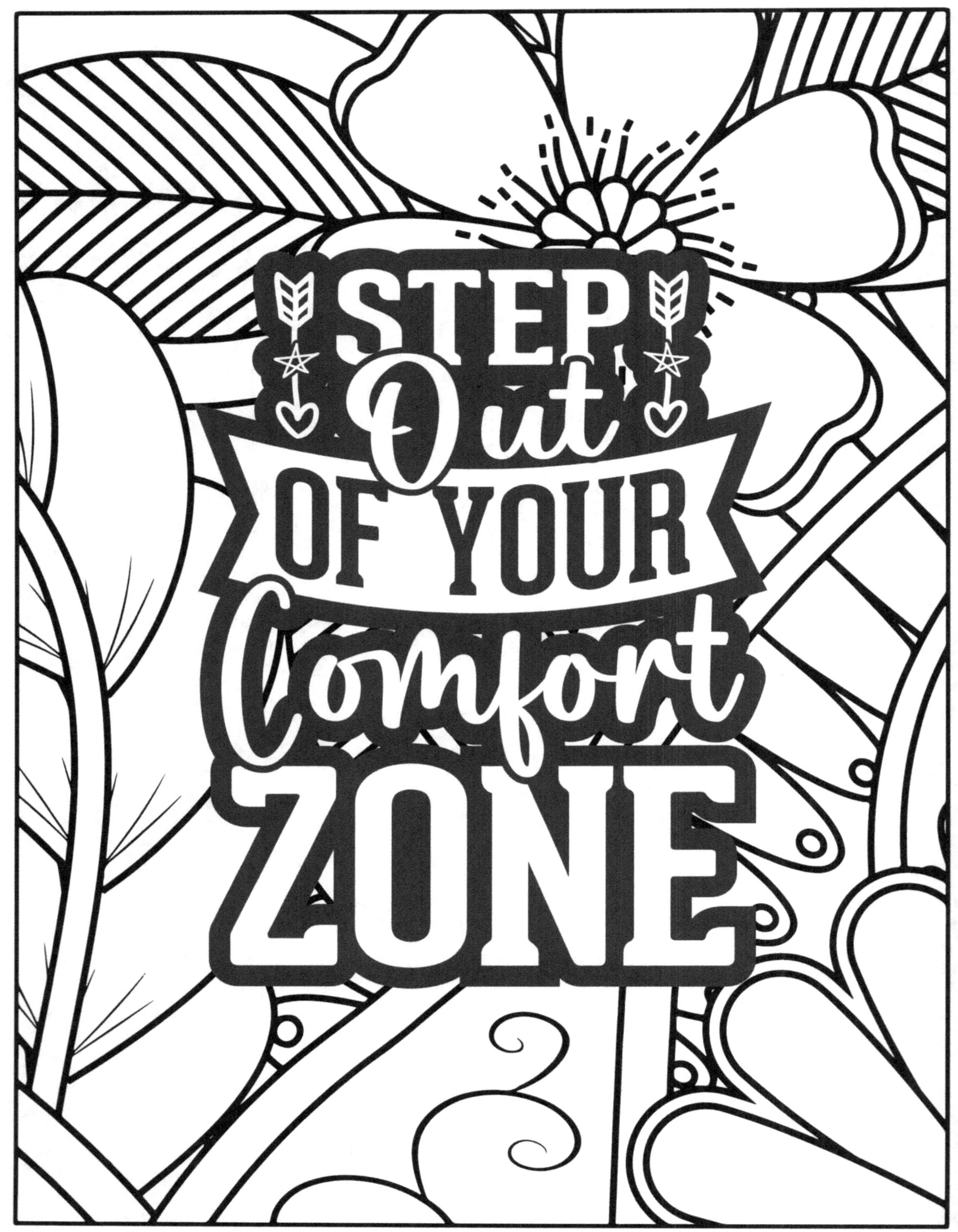

STEP
Out
OF YOUR
Comfort
ZONE

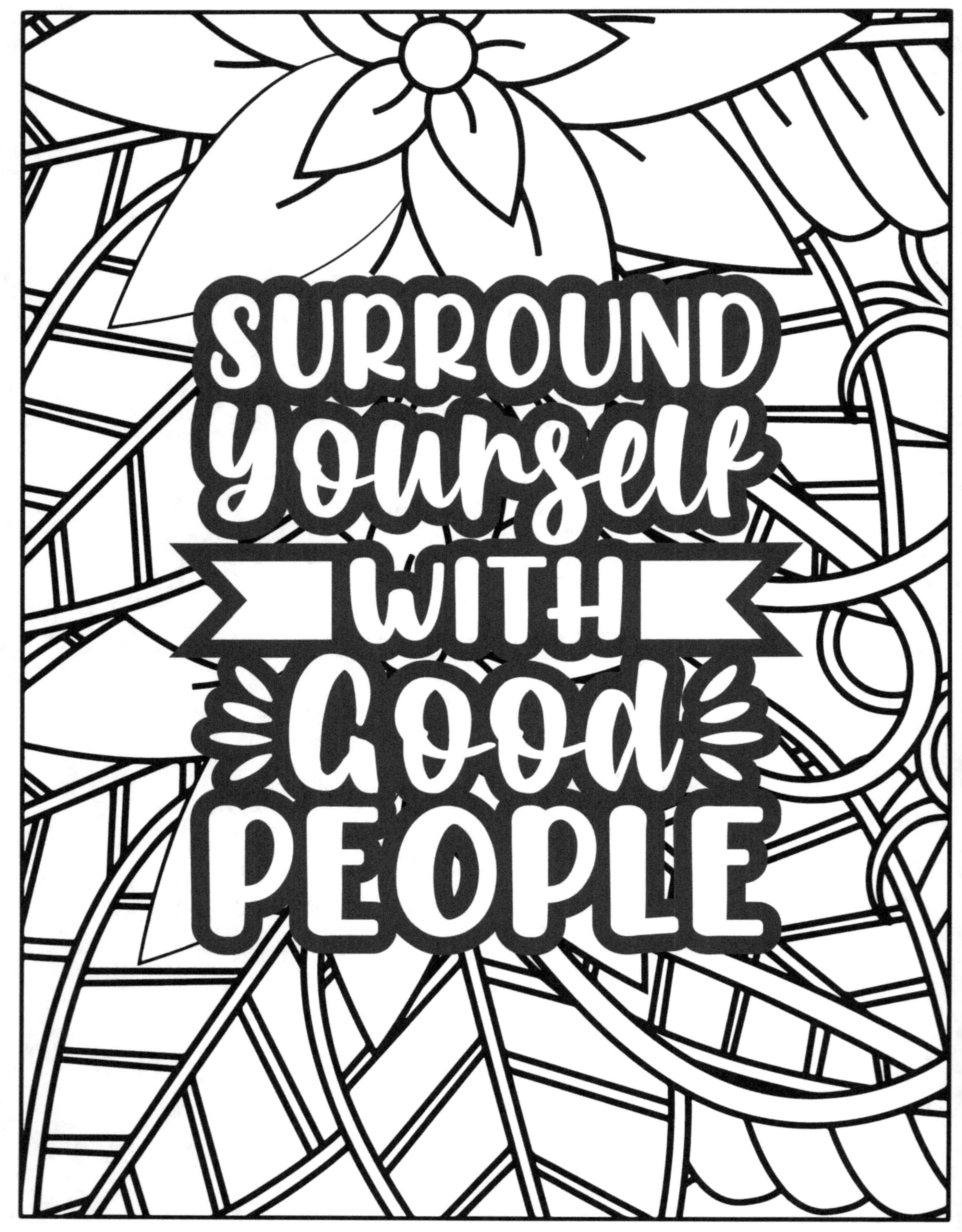

SURROUND YOURSELF WITH GOOD PEOPLE

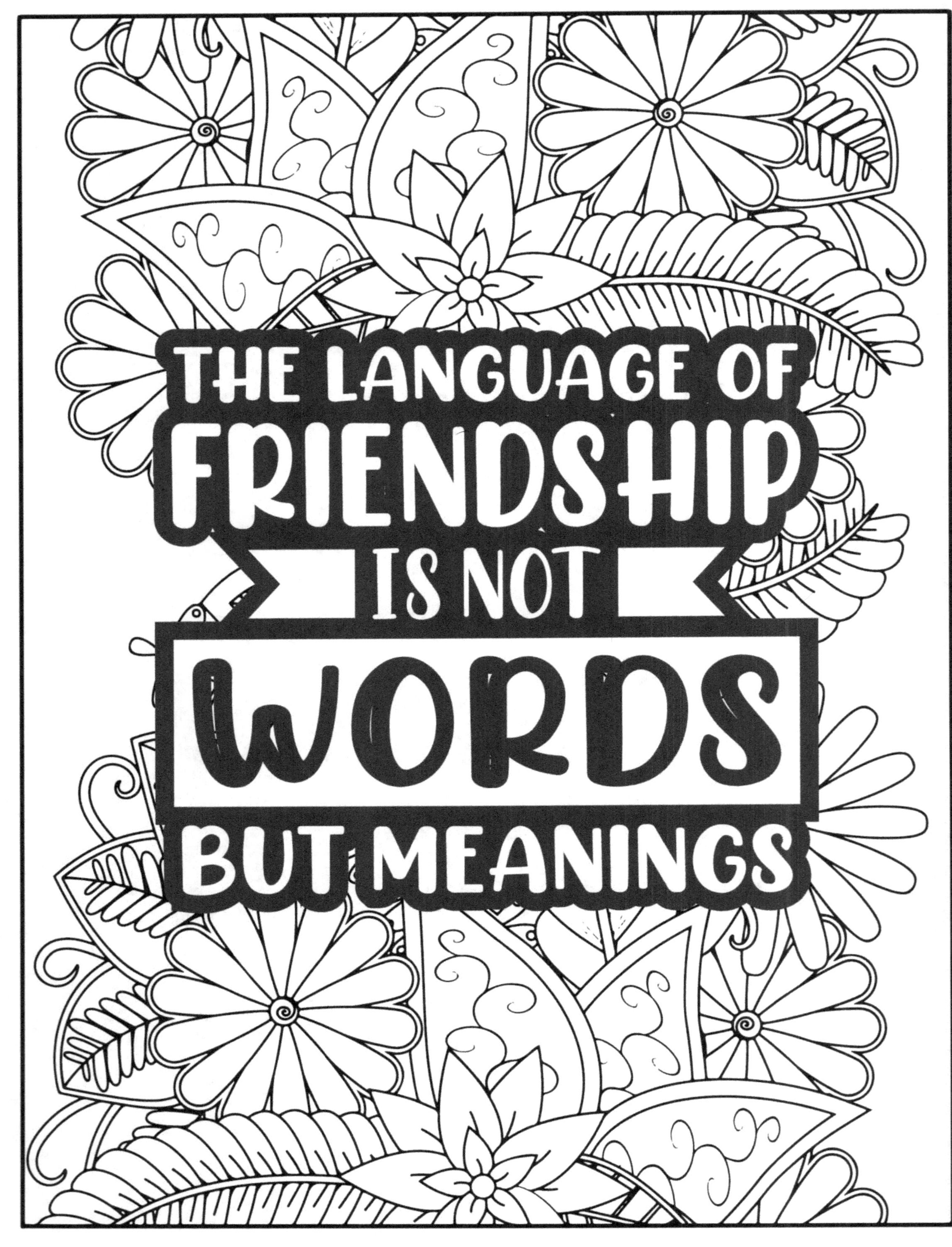

THE LANGUAGE OF
FRIENDSHIP
IS NOT
WORDS
BUT MEANINGS

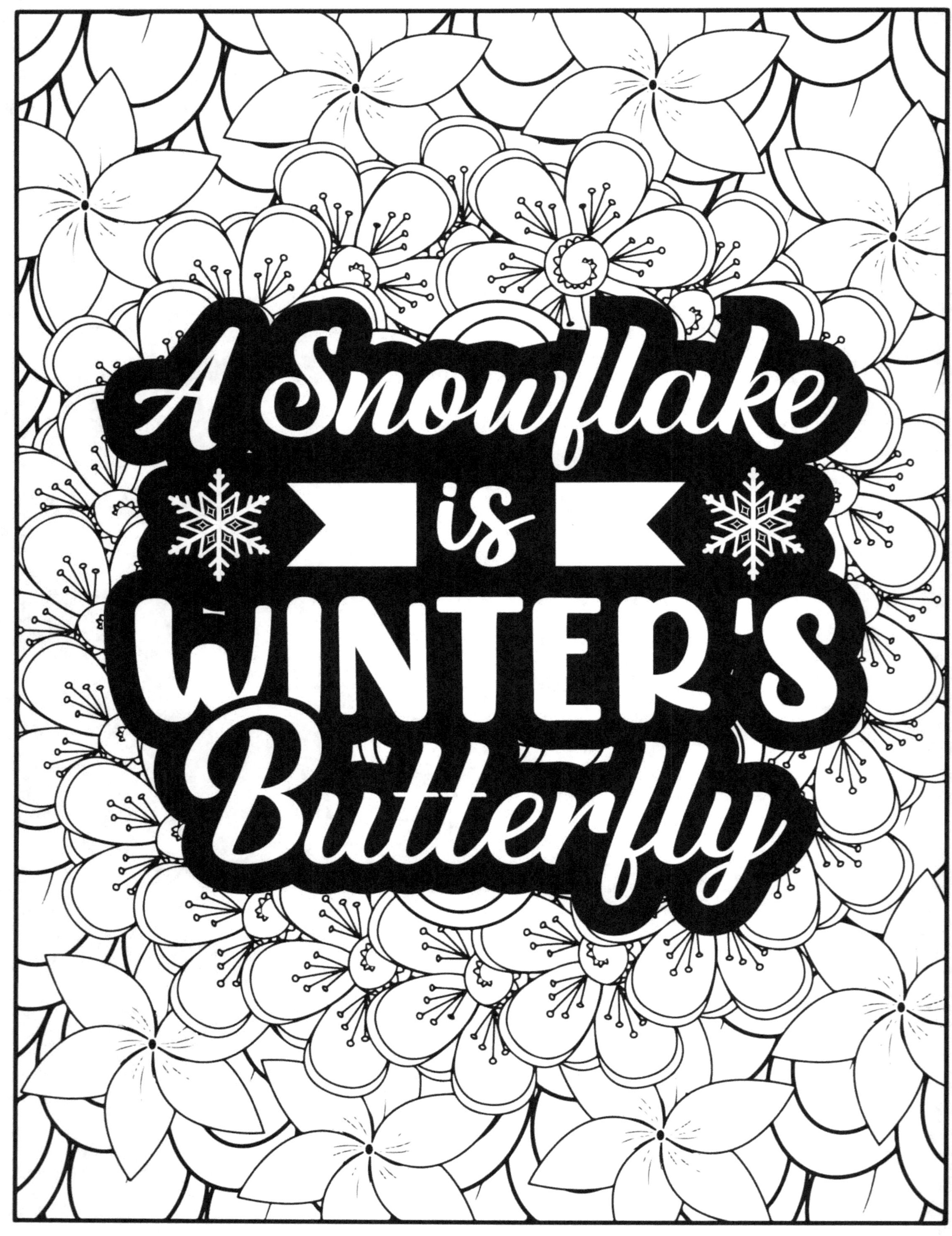

A Snowflake
is
WINTER'S
Butterfly

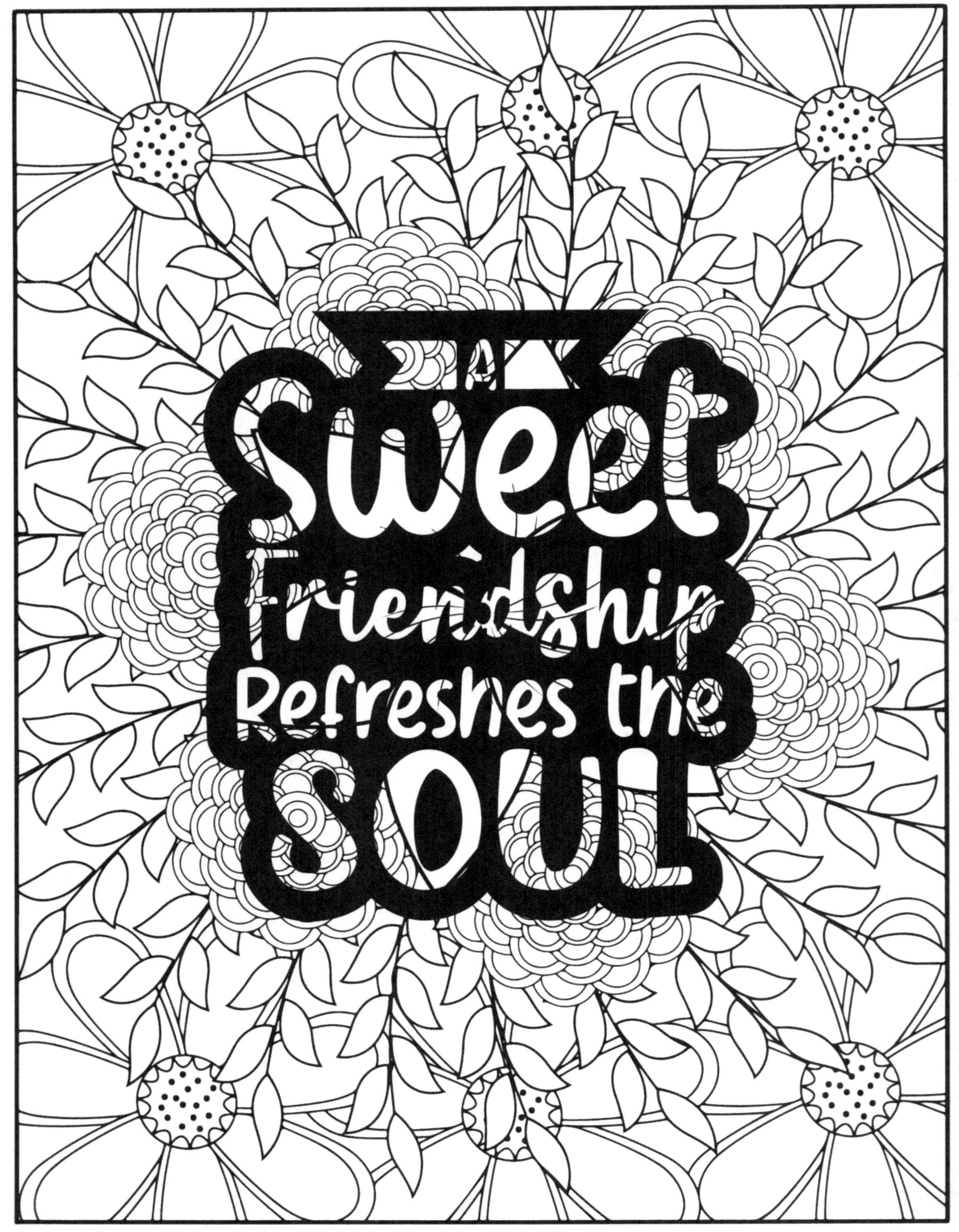

A sweet
Friendship
Refreshes the
SOUL

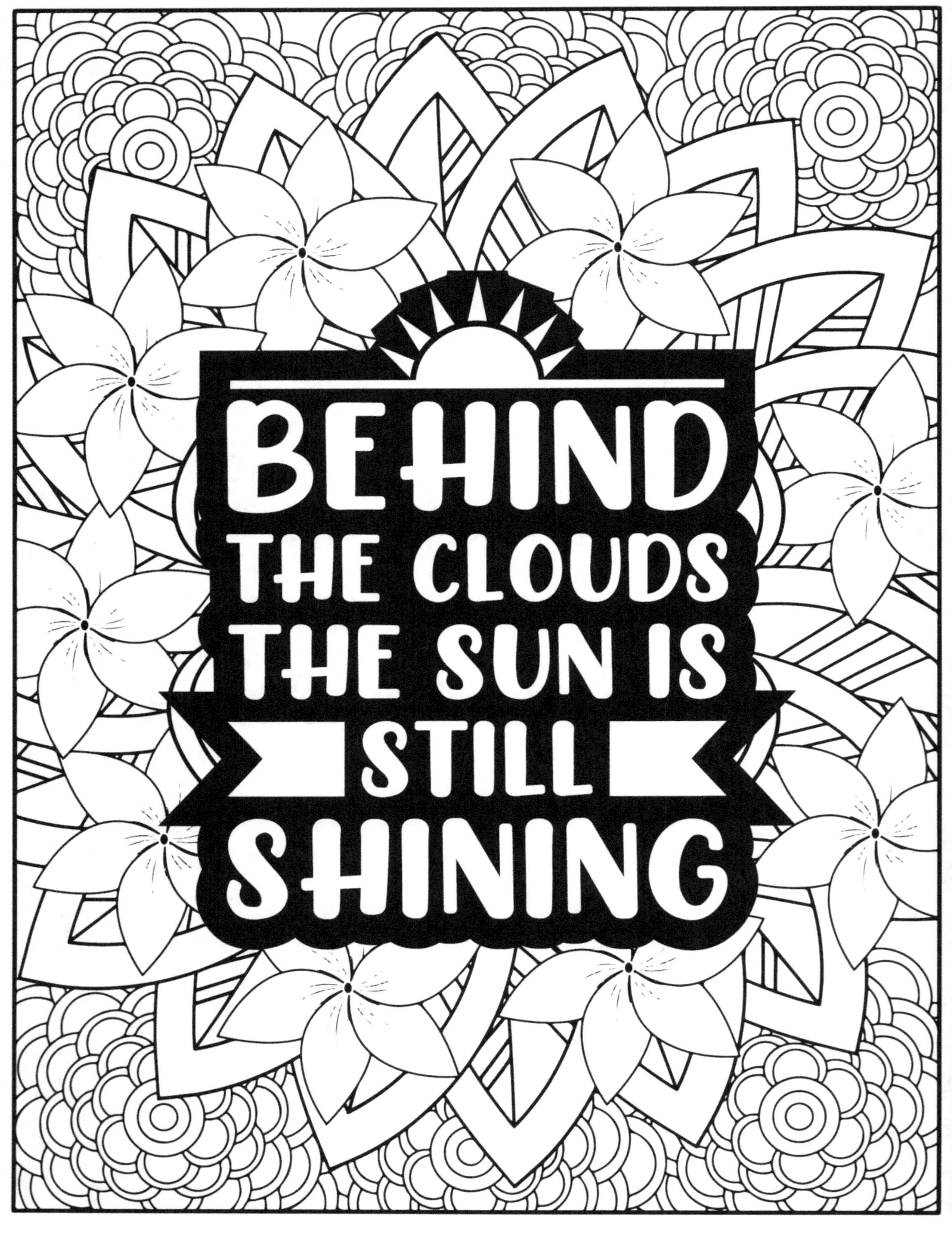

BEHIND
THE CLOUDS
THE SUN IS
STILL
SHINING

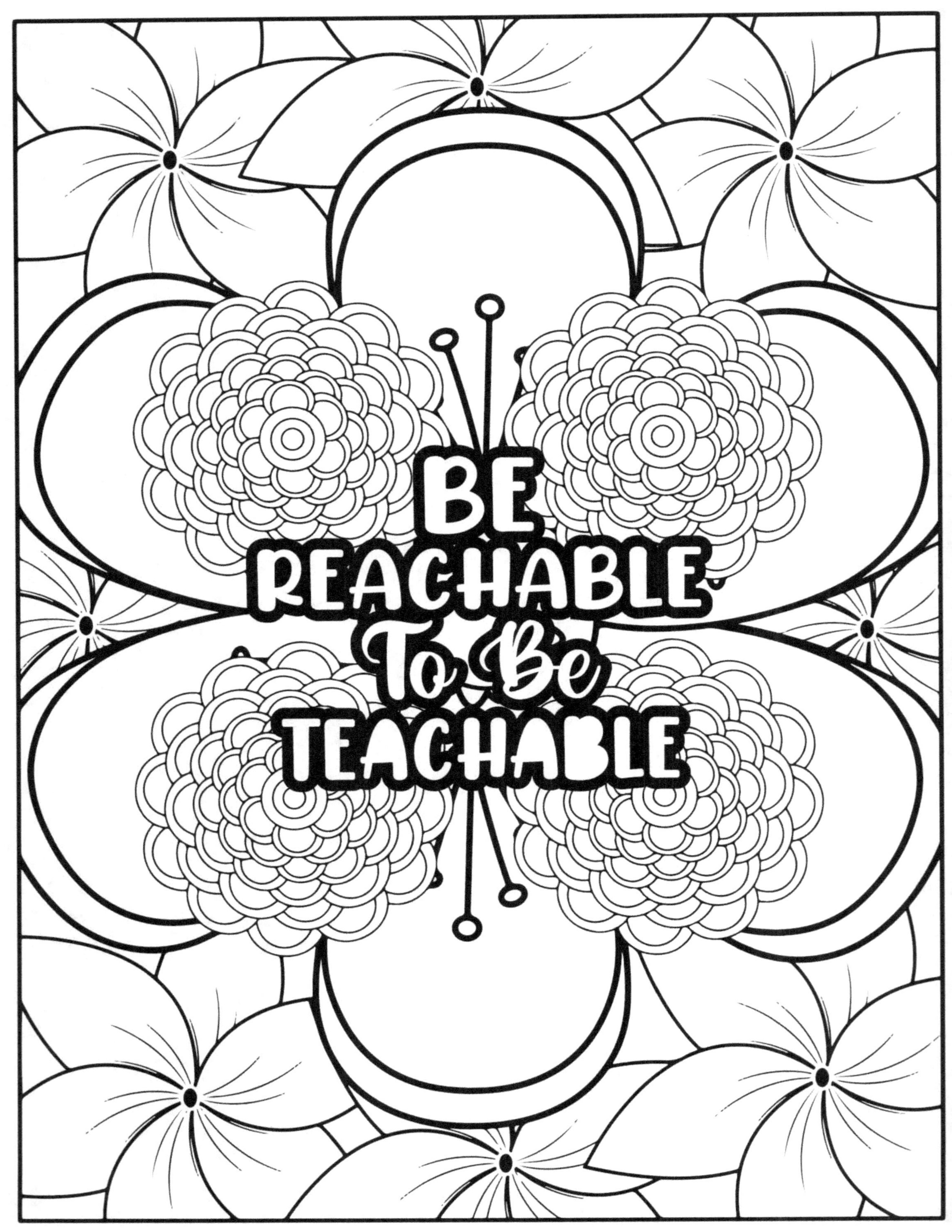

BE
REACHABLE
To Be
TEACHABLE

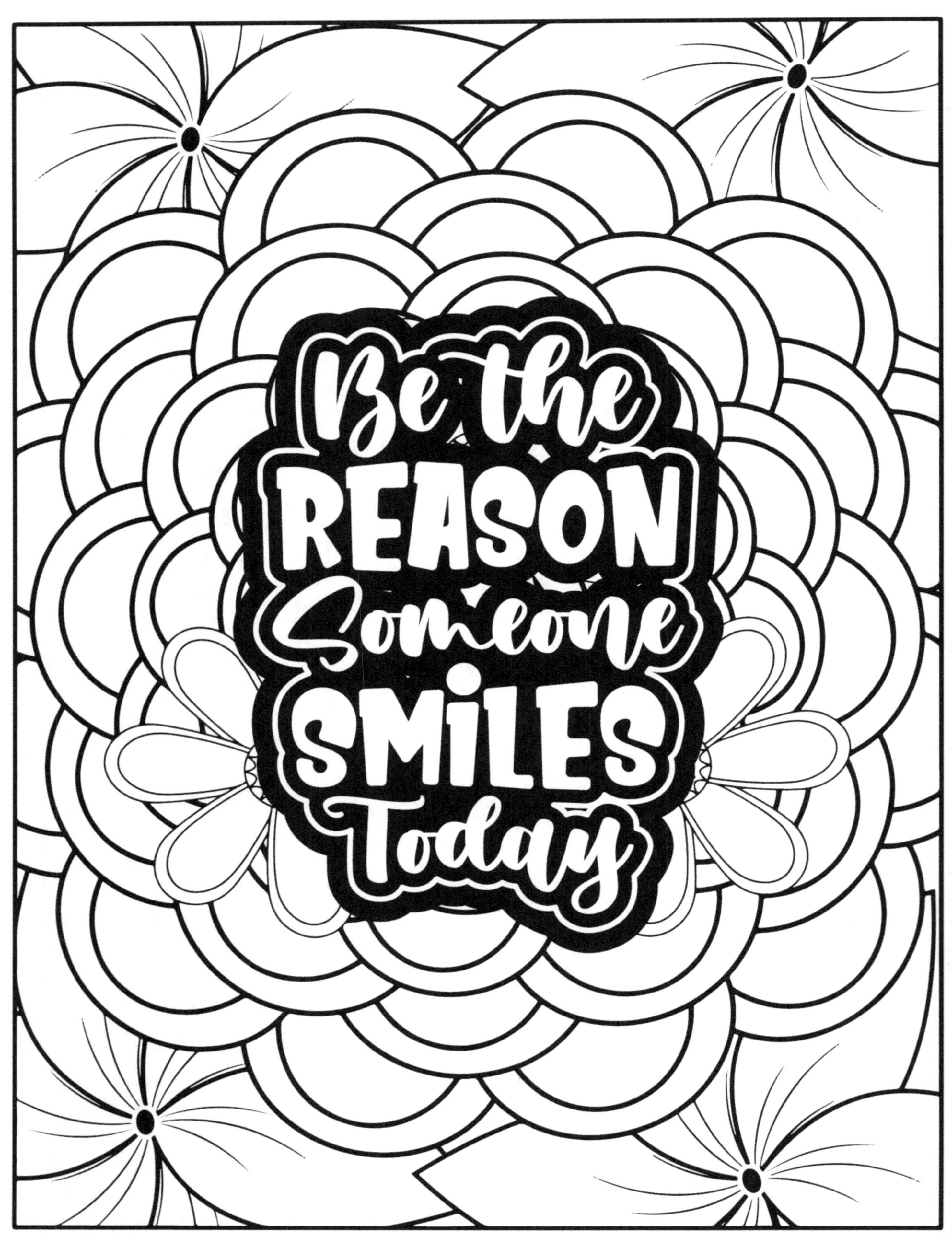

Be the
REASON
Someone
SMILES
Today

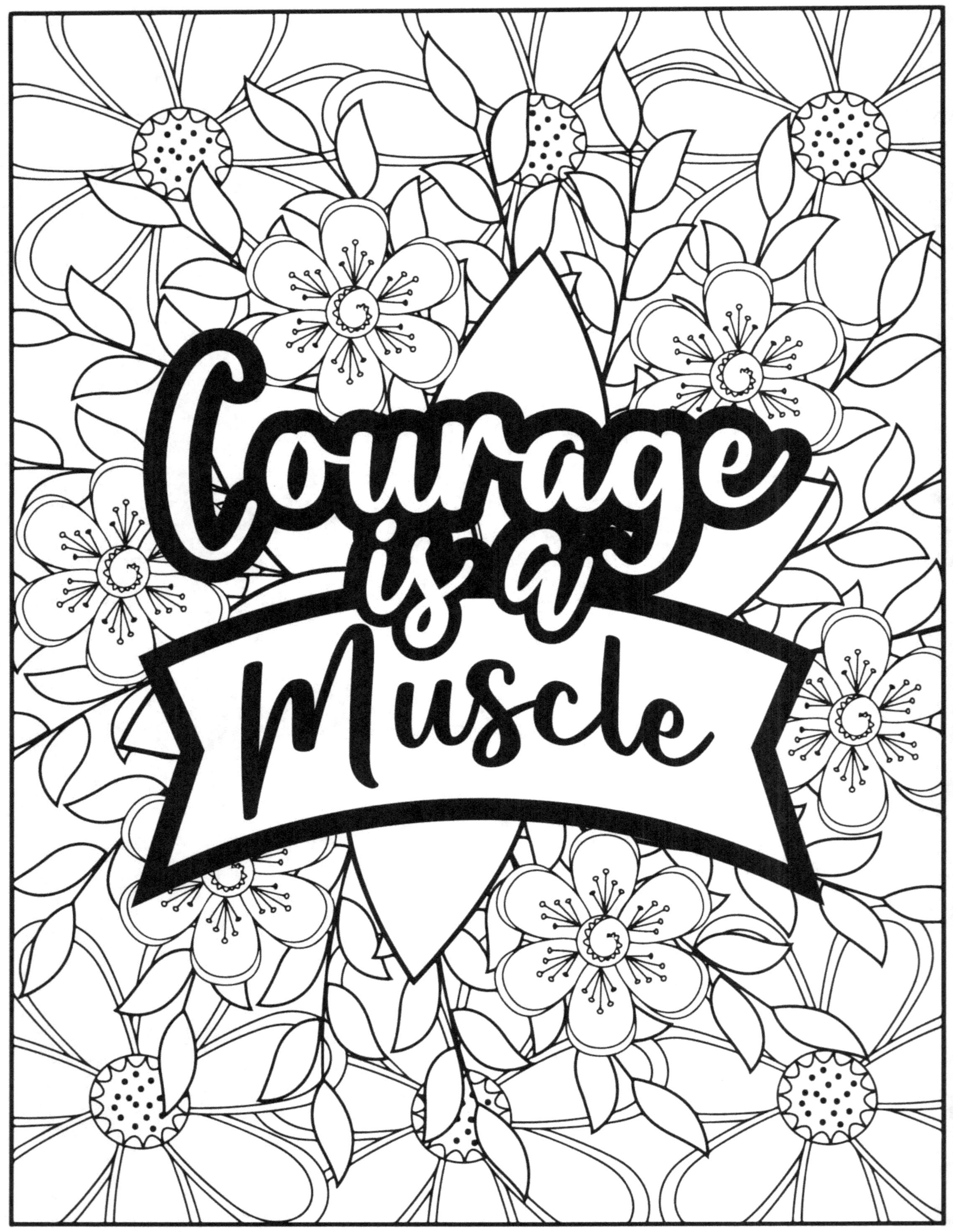

Courage
is a
Muscle

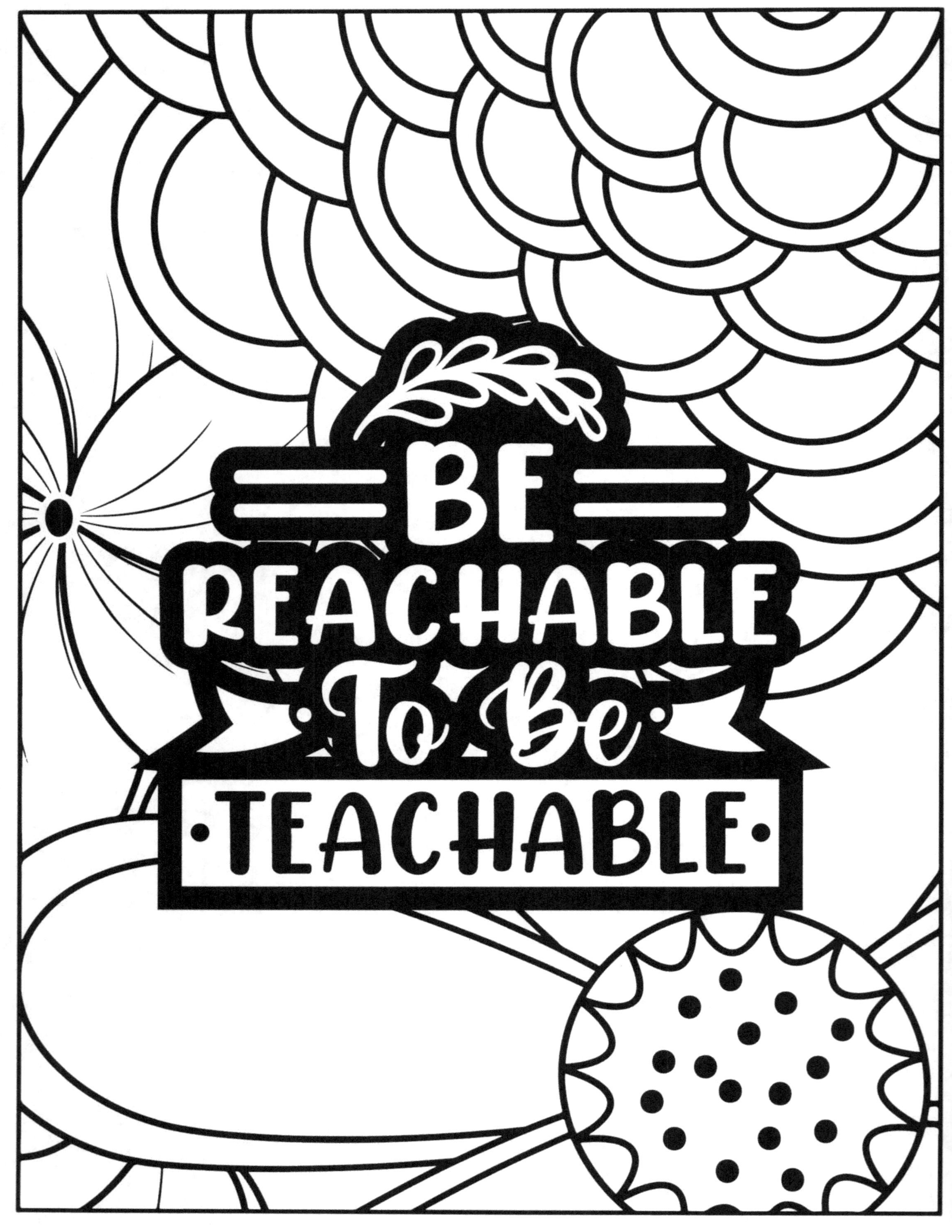
BE
REACHABLE
To Be
TEACHABLE

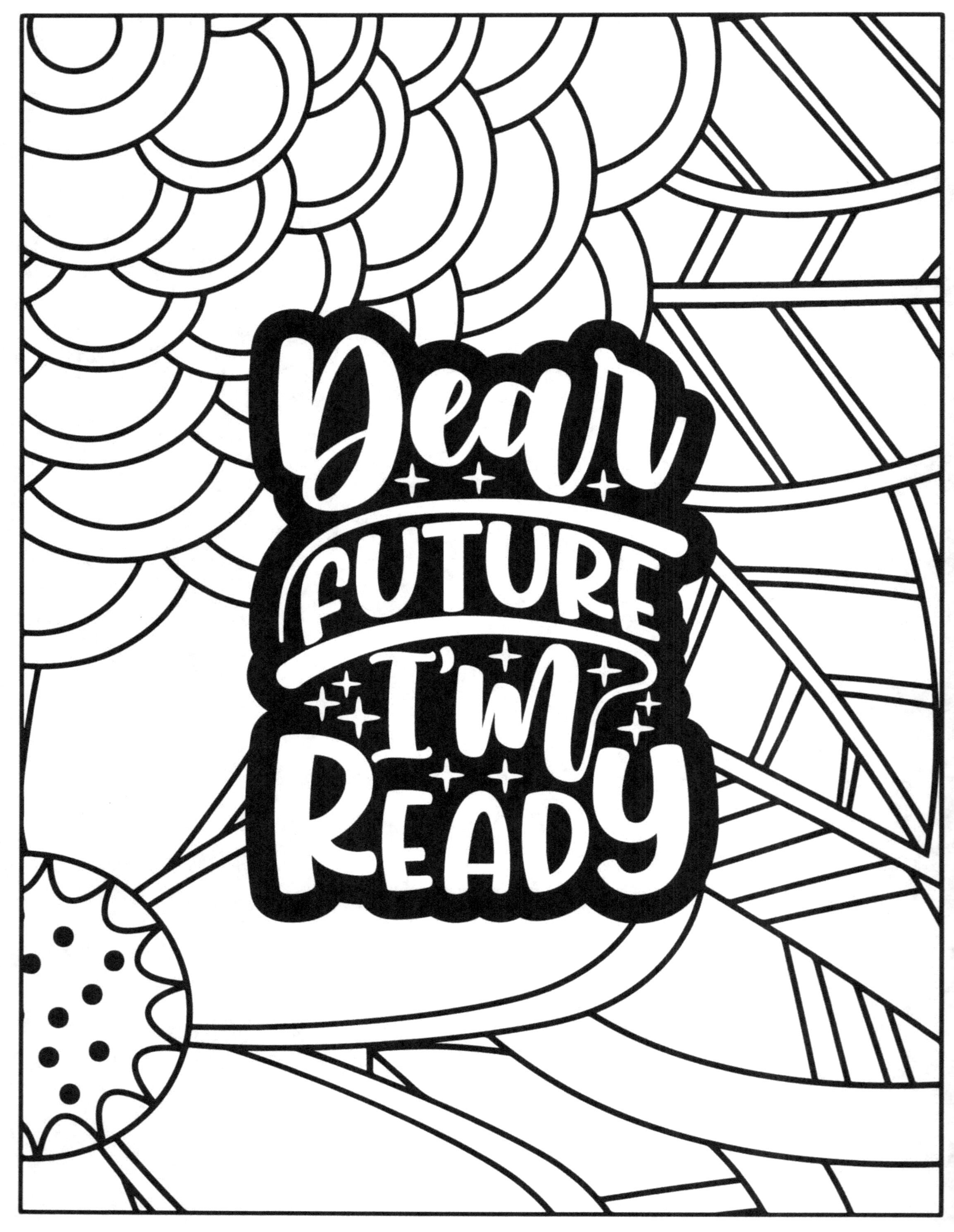
Dear
Future
I'm
Ready

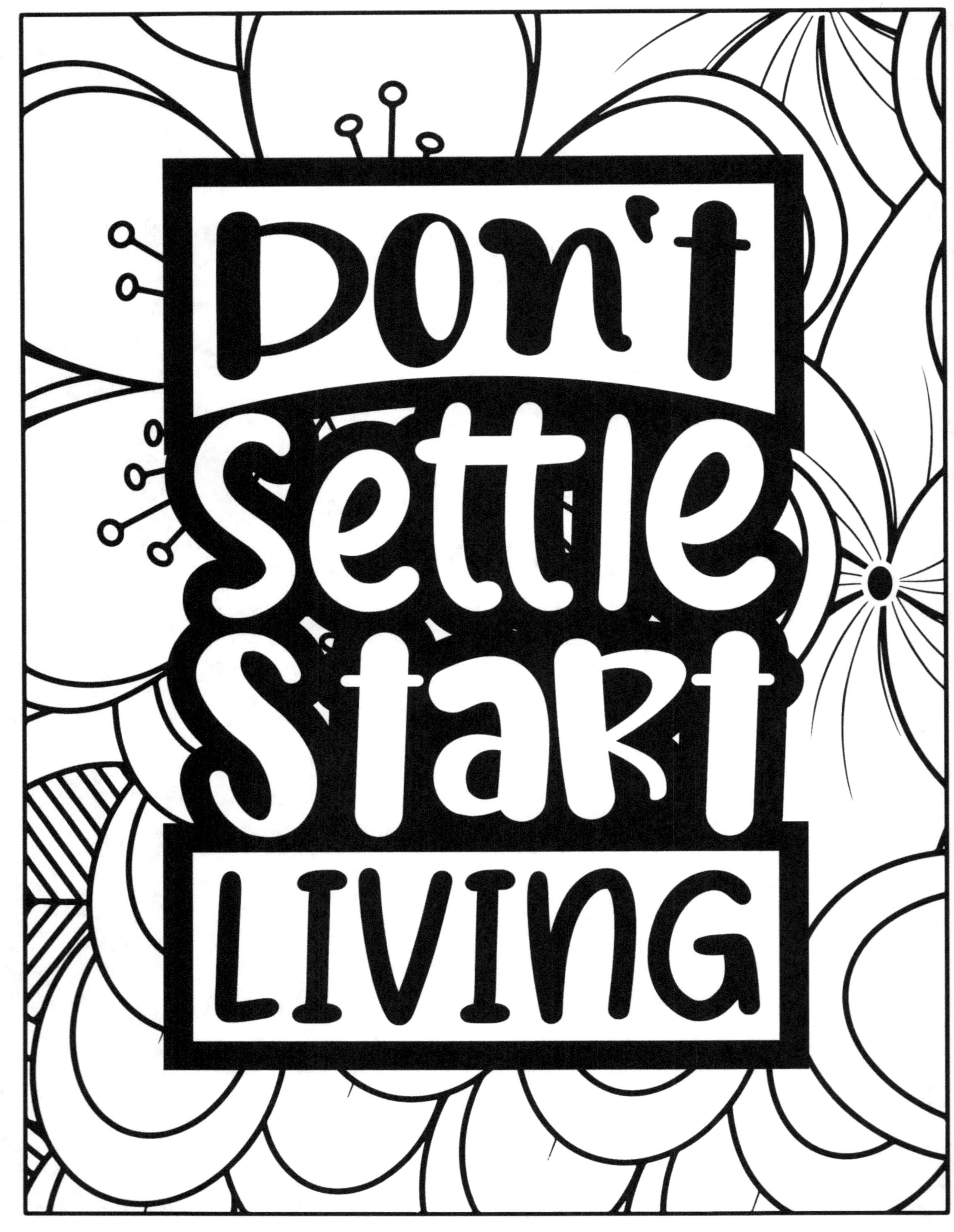

Don't
settle
Start
LIVING

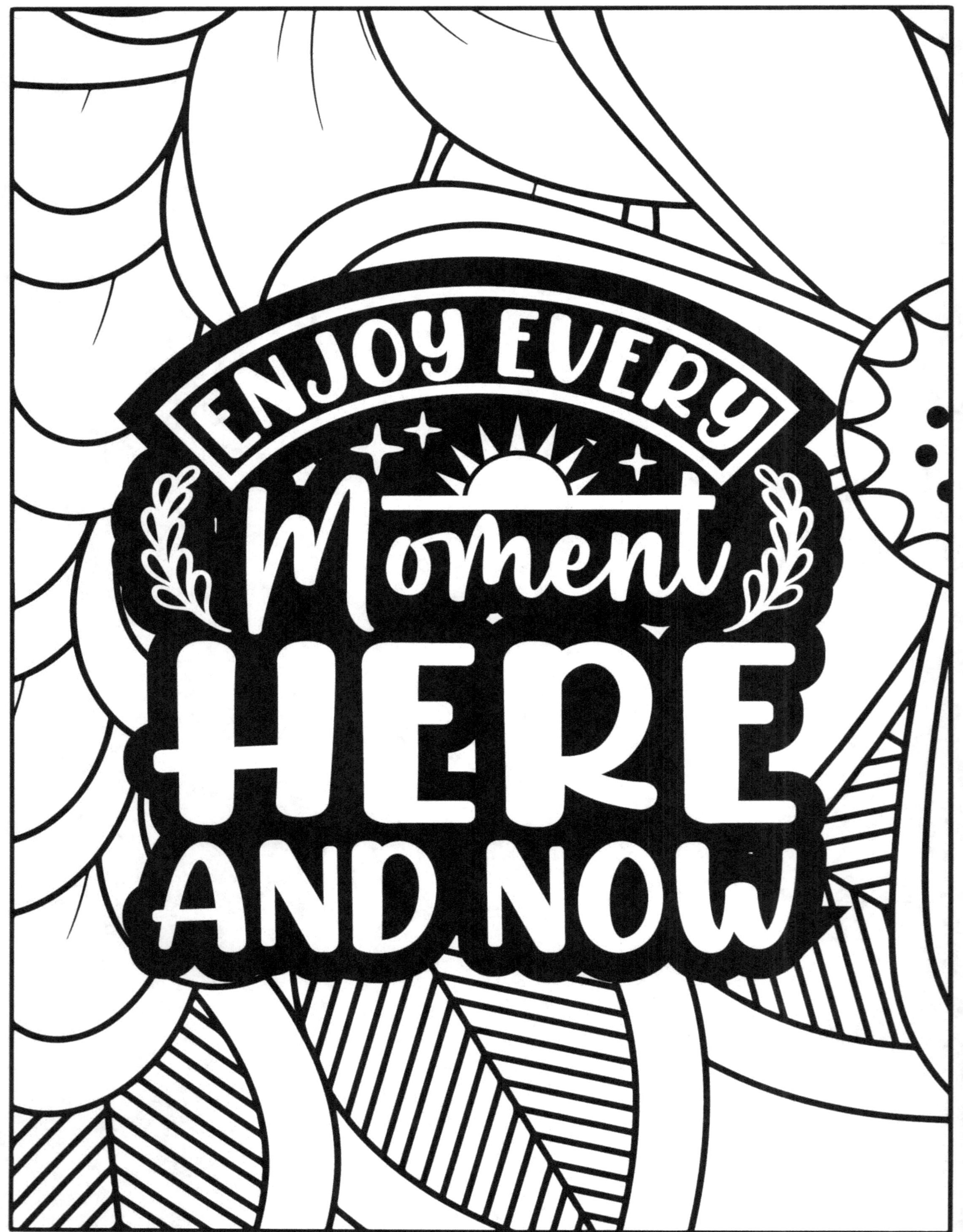

ENJOY EVERY
Moment
HERE
AND NOW

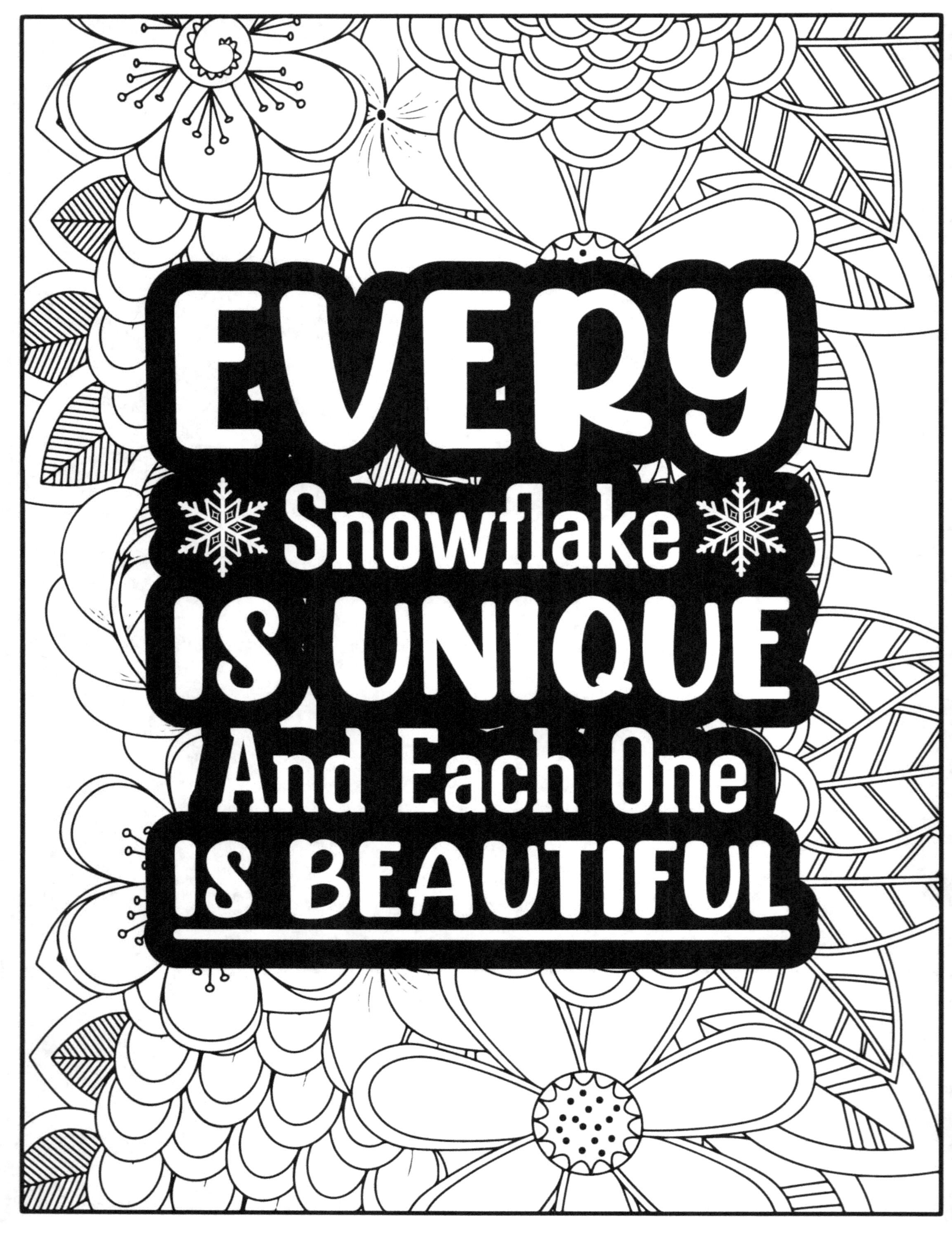

EVERY
Snowflake
IS UNIQUE
And Each One
IS BEAUTIFUL

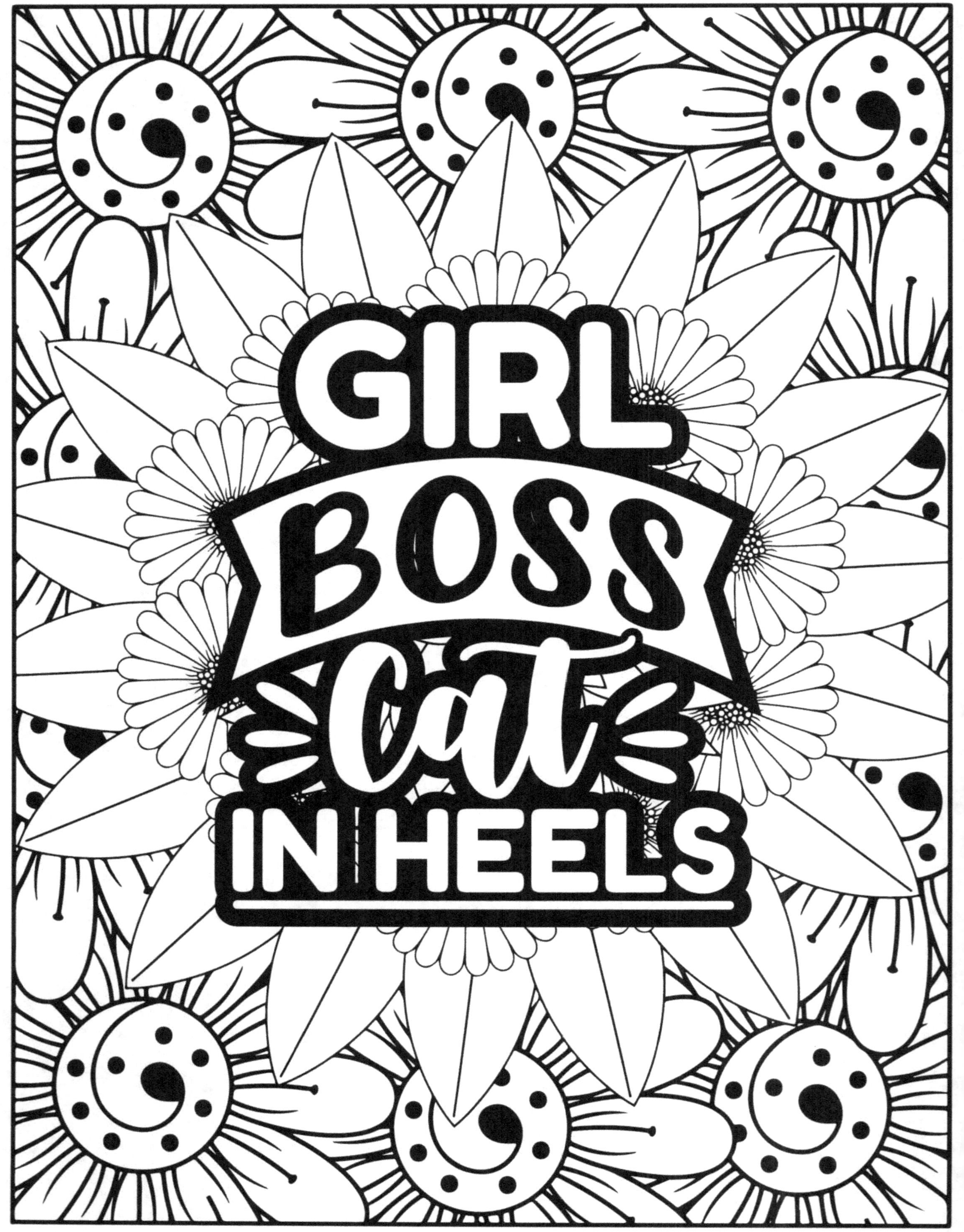

GIRL
BOSS
Cat
IN HEELS

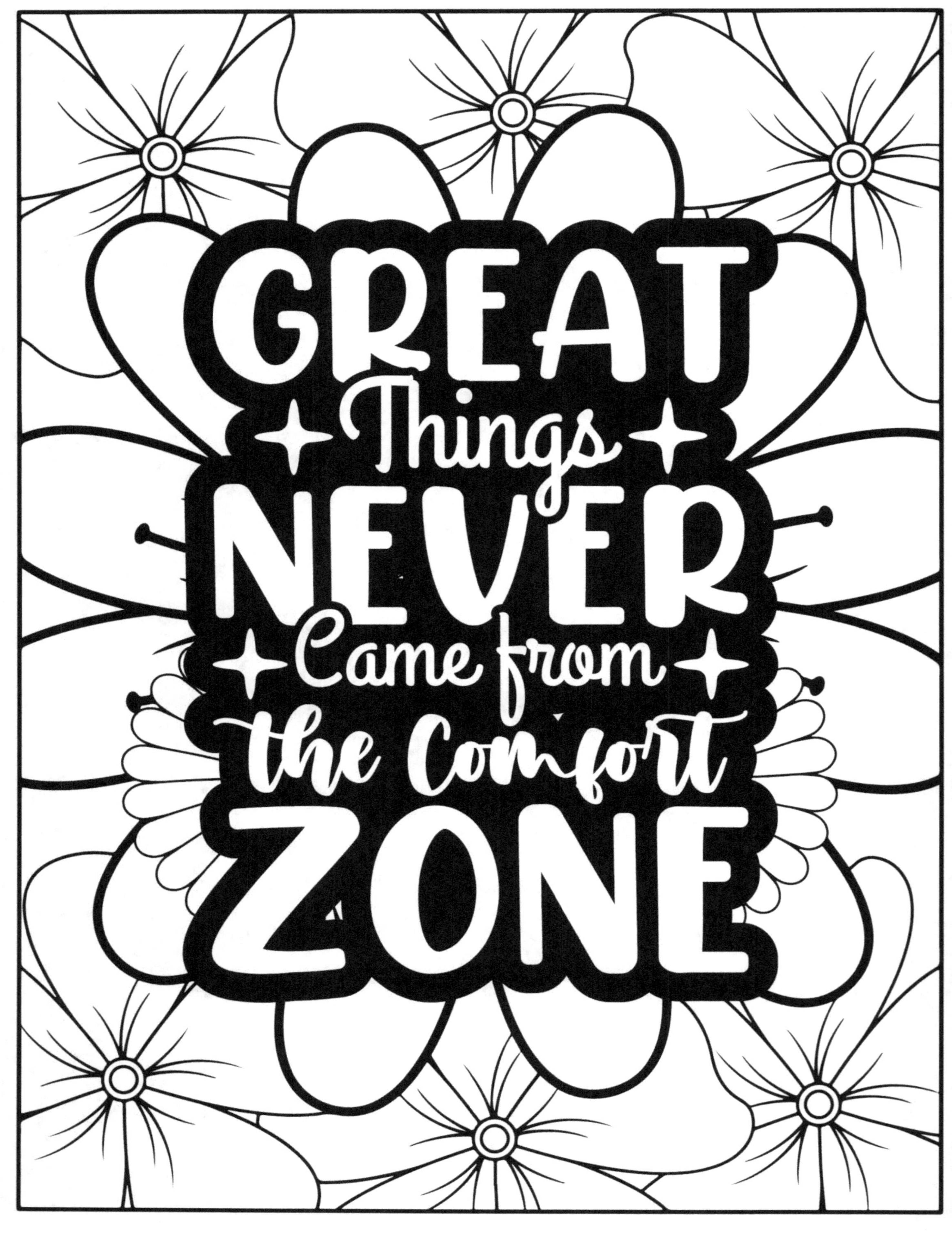

GREAT
Things
NEVER
Came from
the Comfort
ZONE

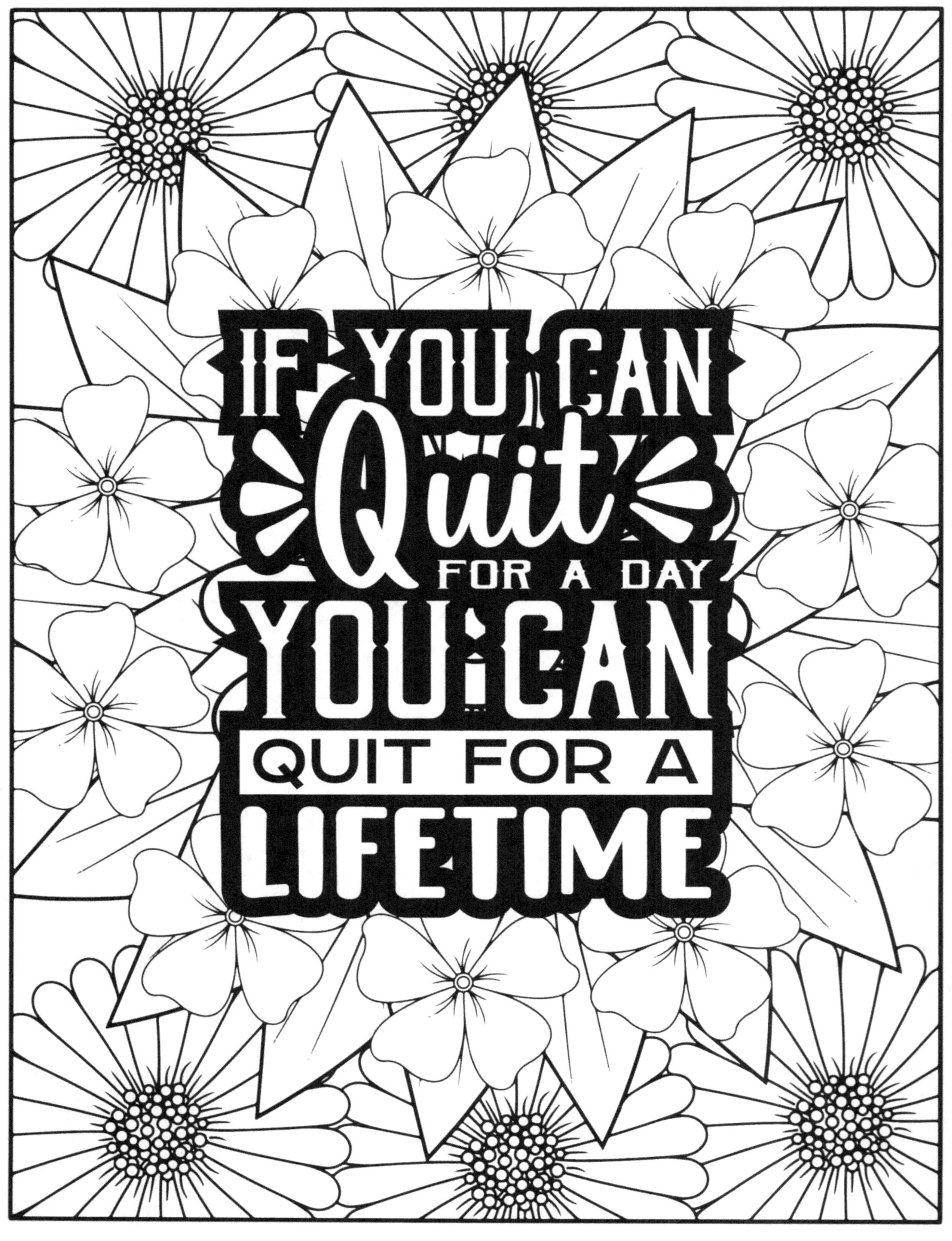

IF YOU CAN
Quit
FOR A DAY
YOU CAN
QUIT FOR A
LIFETIME

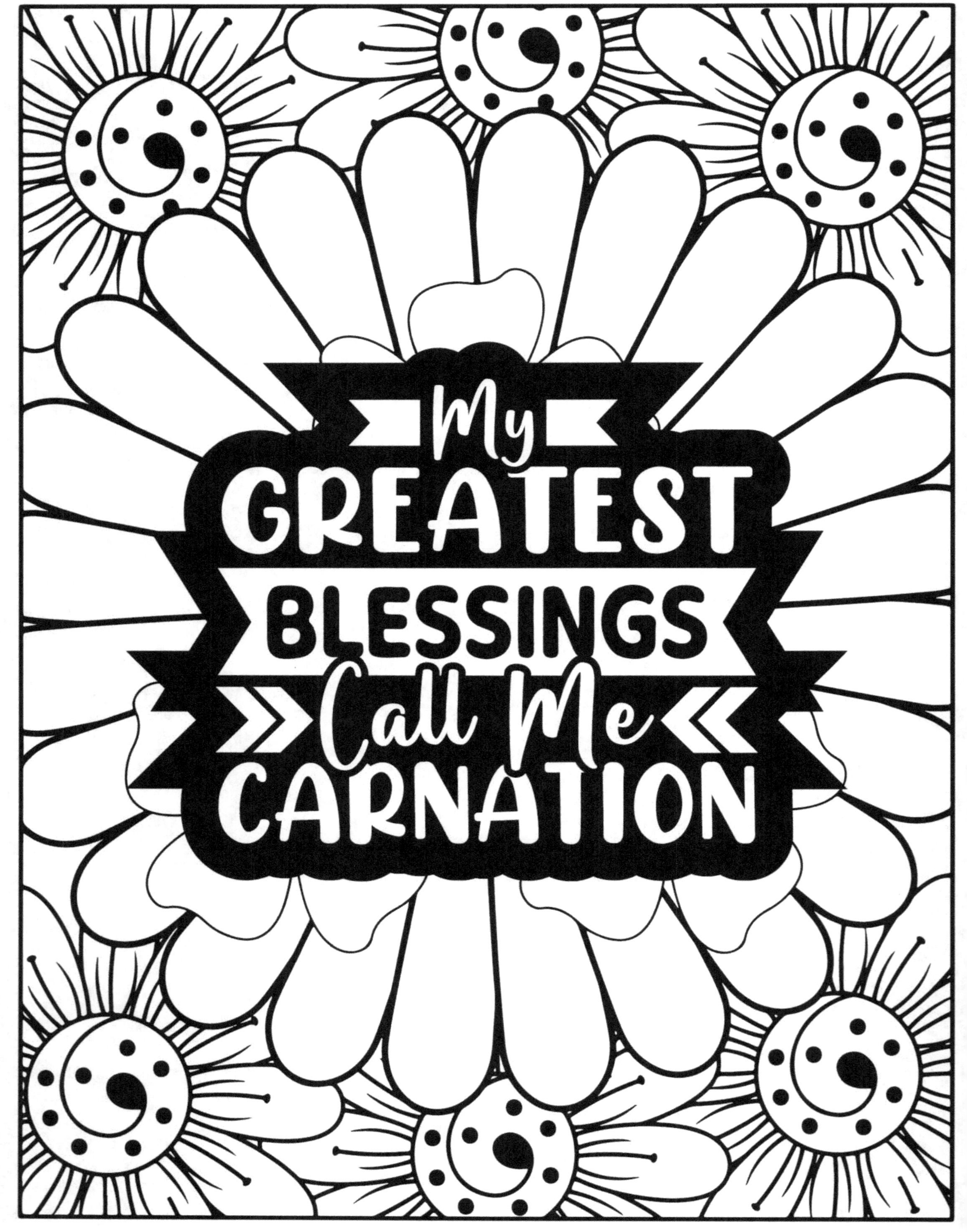

My
GREATEST
BLESSINGS
Call Me
CARNATION

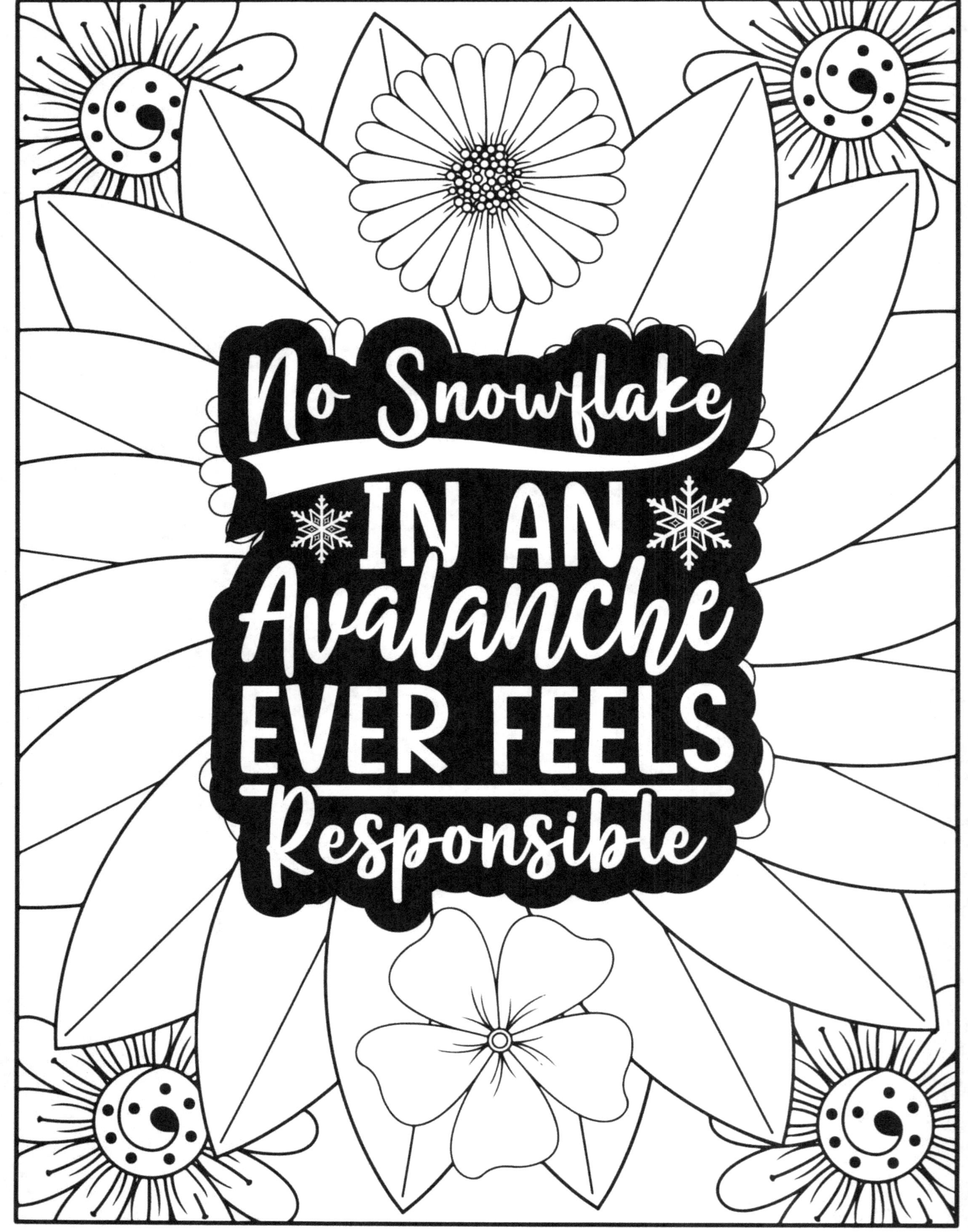

No Snowflake
IN AN
Avalanche
EVER FEELS
Responsible

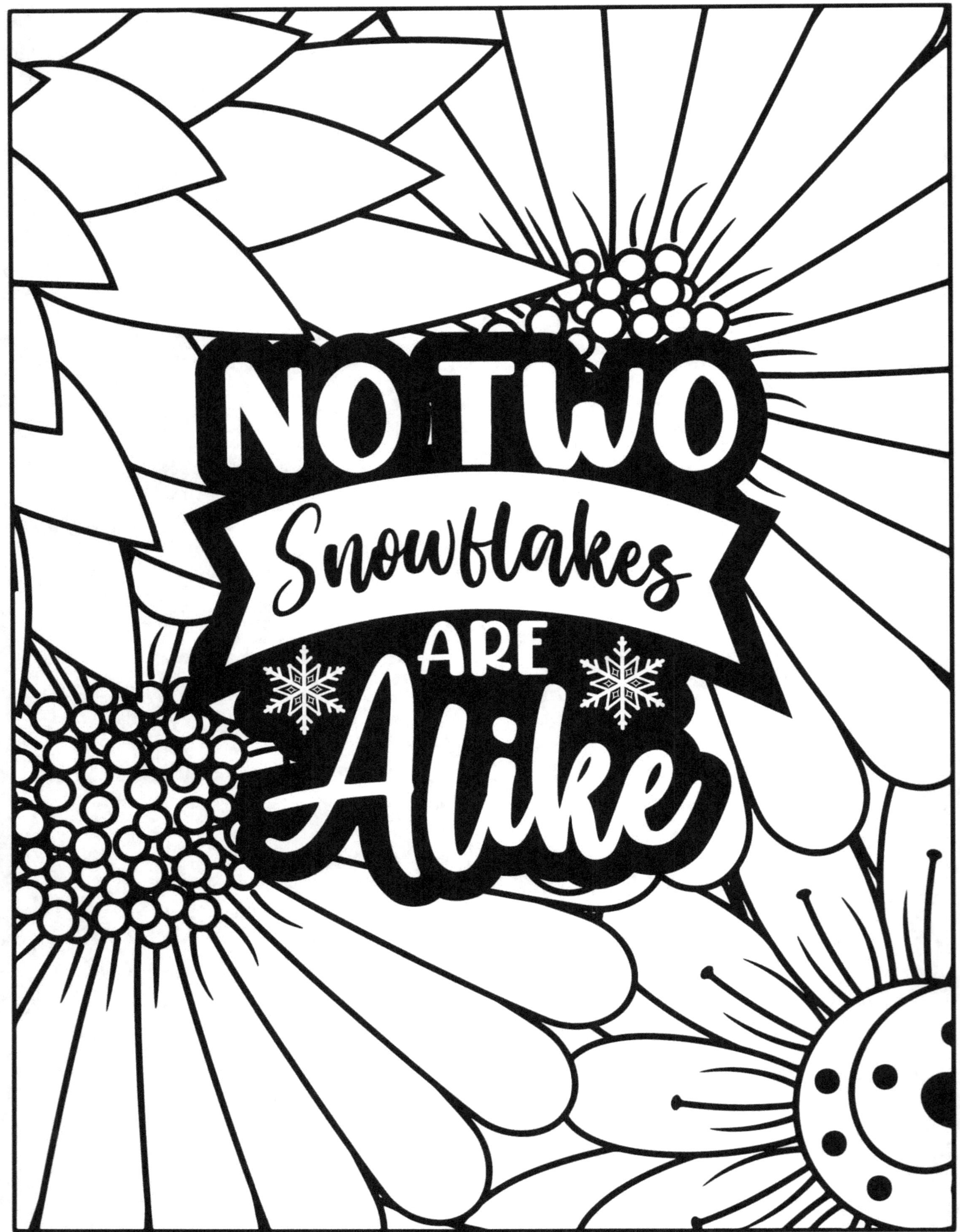

NO TWO
Snowflakes
ARE
Alike

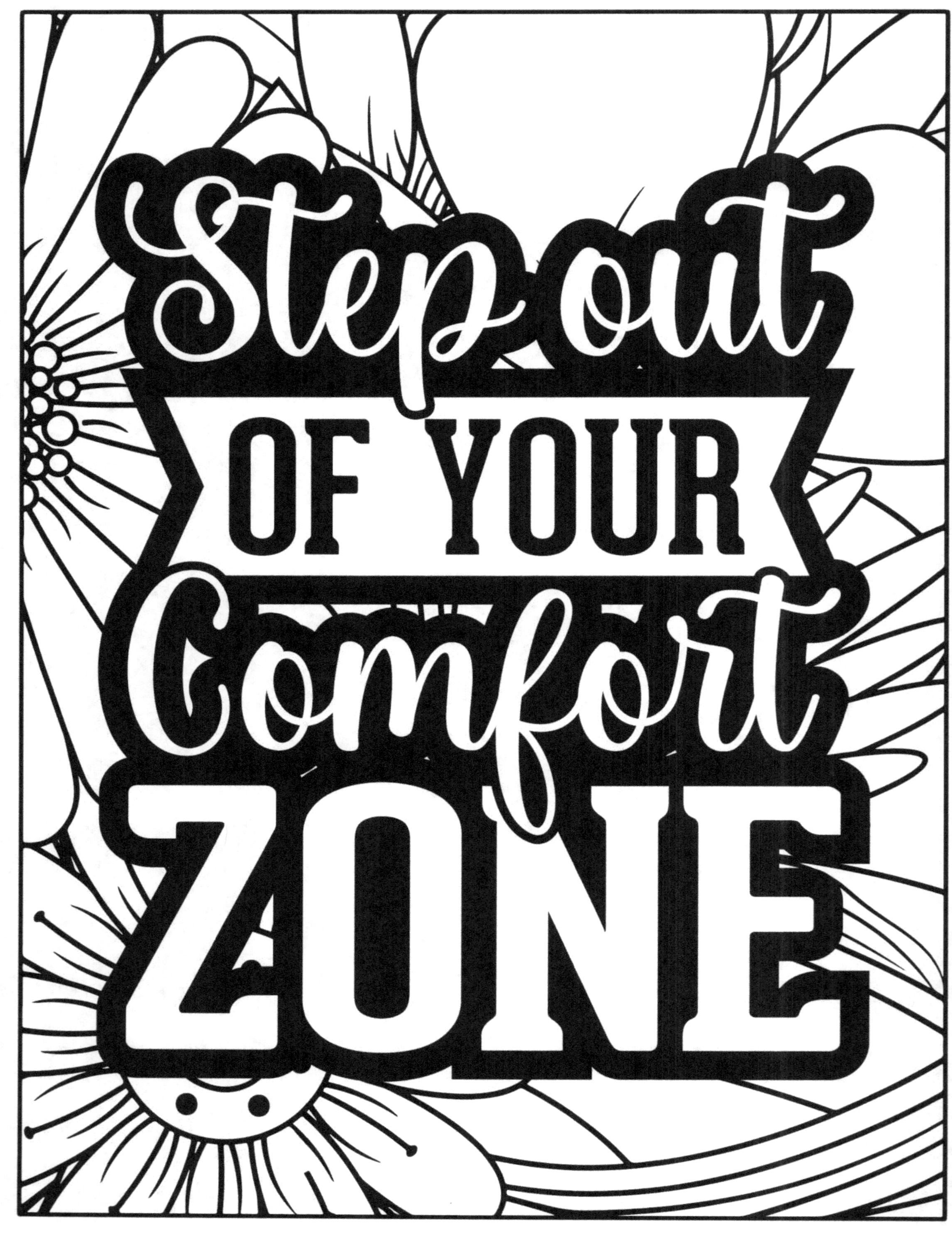

Step out
OF YOUR
Comfort
ZONE

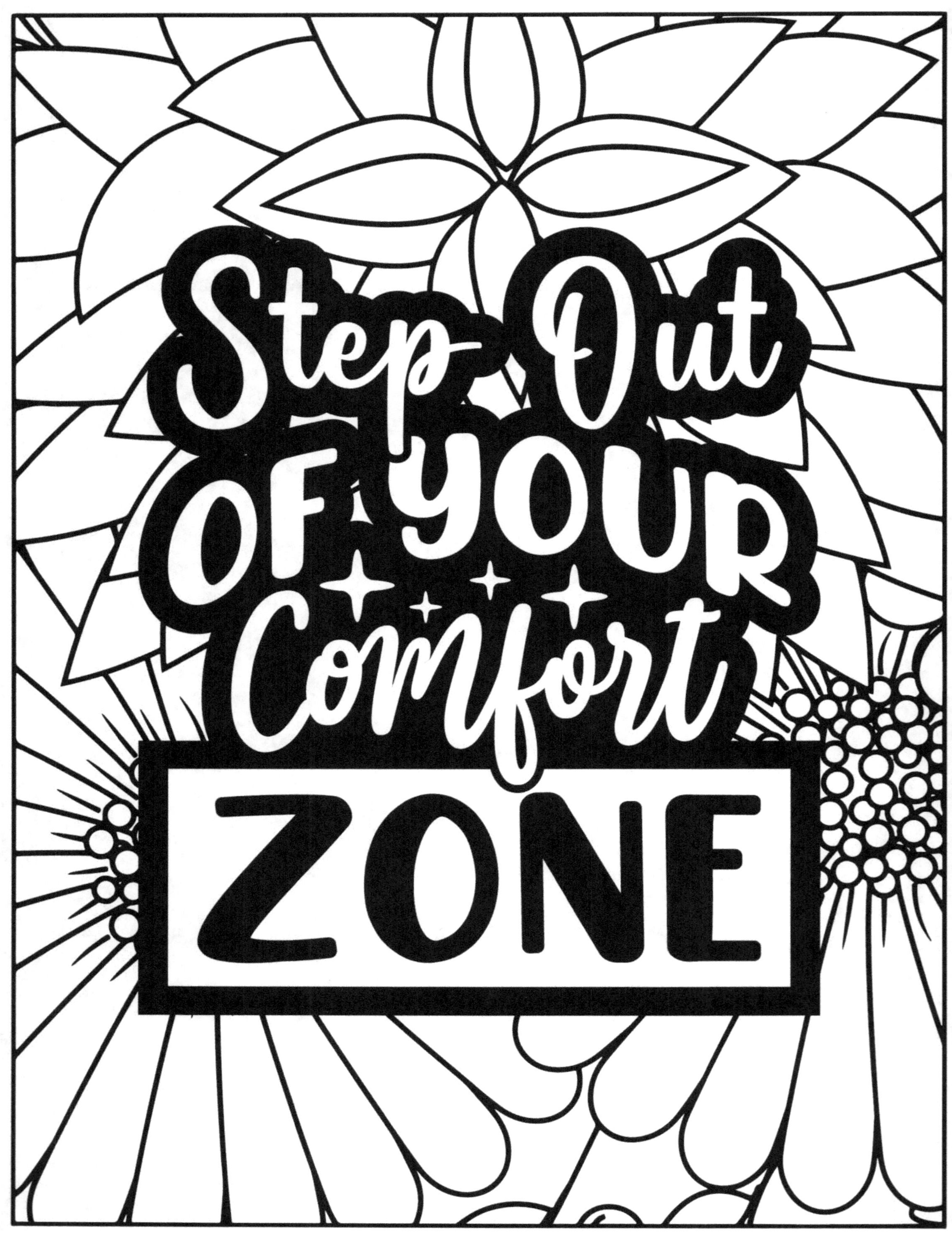

Step Out
OF YOUR
Comfort
ZONE

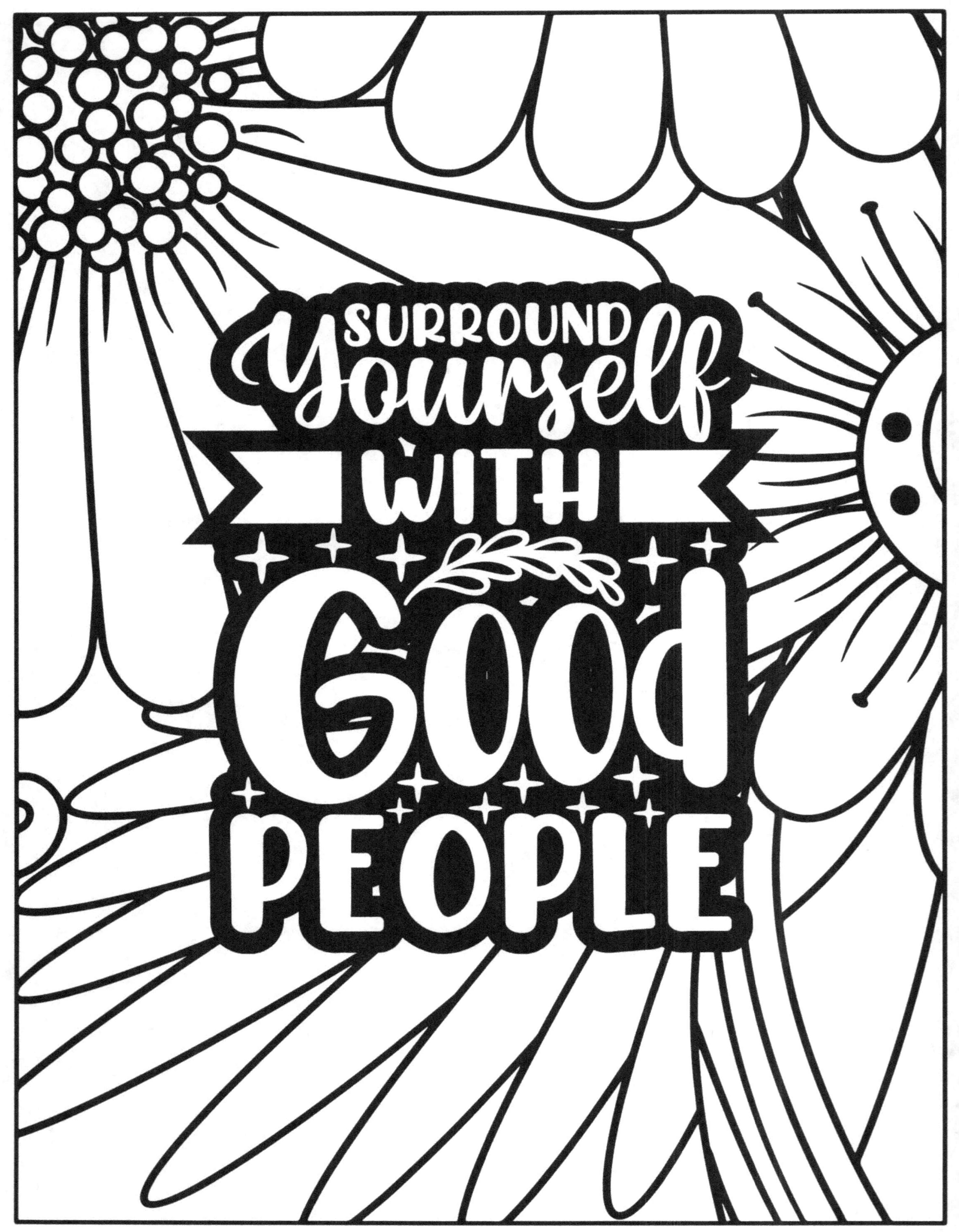

SURROUND
Yourself
WITH
Good
PEOPLE

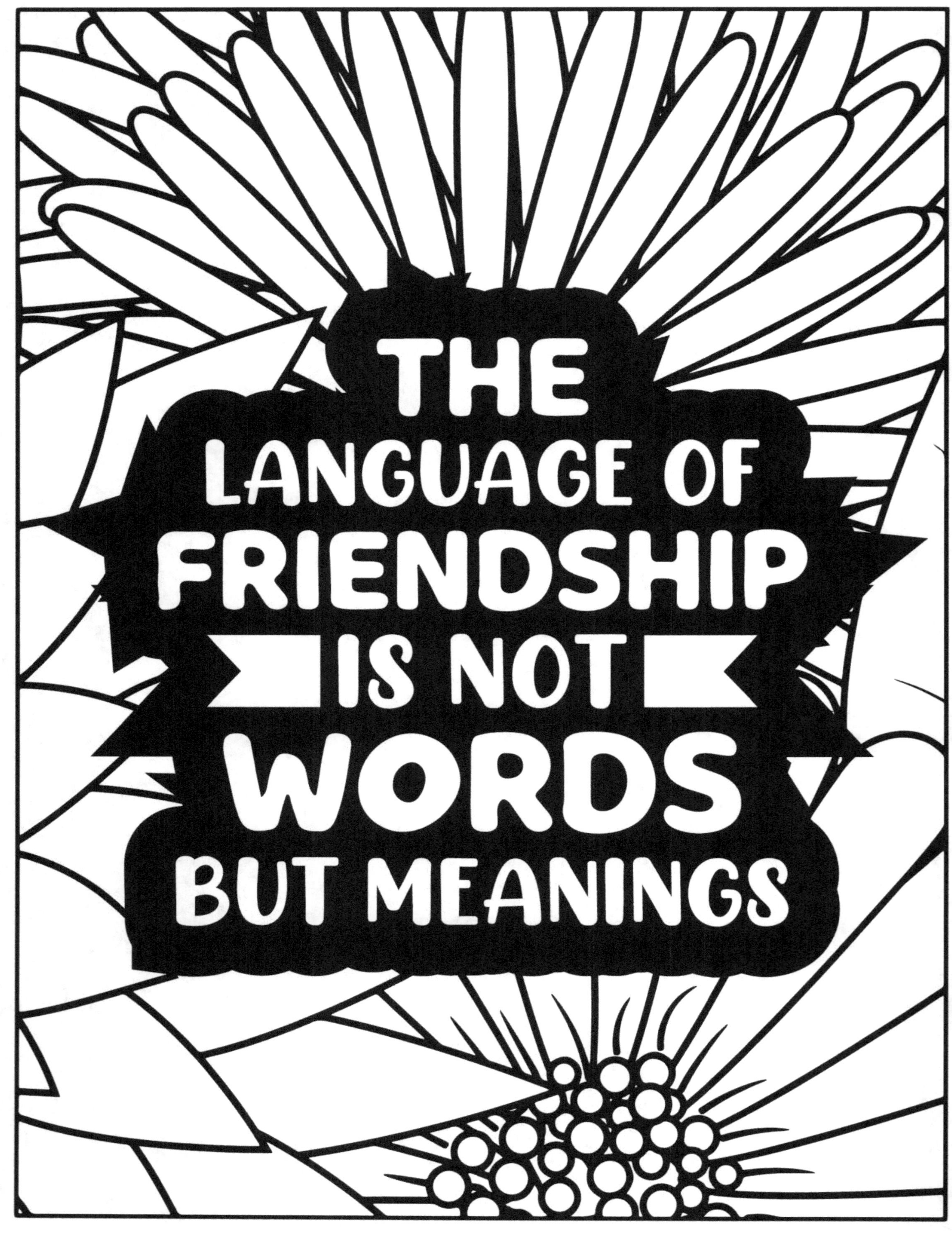

THE
LANGUAGE OF
FRIENDSHIP
IS NOT
WORDS
BUT MEANINGS